THE PROOFREADER'S GUIDE TO COMIC BOOK STYLE

Text and graphics © 2024 Madeleine Vasaly
www.madeleinevasaly.com

All rights reserved. Except in the case of brief quotations in reviews and certain other noncommercial uses permitted by copyright law, no part of this publication may be reproduced, distributed, or transmitted in any form without a team license or other form of prior written permission. For more information, contact hello@madeleinevasaly.com. Published in Minneapolis, Minnesota, USA.

10 9 8 7 6 5 4 3 2 1

ISBN-13:
979-8-9901170-1-3 (paperback)
979-8-9901170-0-6 (PDF)
979-8-9901170-2-0 (epub)

Library of Congress Control Number: 2024918899

Copyeditor: Scott Pearson
Proofreader: Heidi Ward
Cover and Layout Designer: Cindy Samargia Laun

Lettering fonts and brushes by Blambot and Comicraft.

Thank you to Tanya Gold, J. M. Lee, Bailey Harrington, Steve Colle, and everyone else who provided feedback on this book in its various stages, and to Allyson Rudolph and Brett Hallahan at DC Comics for an unbeatable comics proofreading education.

THE PROOFREADER'S GUIDE TO COMIC BOOK STYLE

AN EDITORIAL HANDBOOK FOR PRINT AND DIGITAL COMICS

MADELEINE VASALY

CONTENTS

Introduction — 6
What I Mean by "Comics" — 8
Who This Book Is For — 8
Notes on Terminology — 11

1 Editing, Proofreading, and the Comics Workflow — 14
Workflow Overview — 16
The Role(s) of the Editor — 21
The Role(s) of the Proofreader — 27

2 Editorial Style — 30
What Is Style? — 31
How to Use This Chapter — 34
Capitalization — 35
Punctuation — 40
Numbers — 54
Formatting — 57
Captions, Notes, and Bursts — 65
Special Symbols — 69
Spelling — 72

3. Copyediting Scripts — 79
The Case for Copyediting — 81
Copyediting Scope — 82
Script Format — 84
Editing Tips — 90

4. Proofreading Layouts and Lettering — 94
What Is Lettering? — 95
What Is Typesetting? — 96
Proofreading Scope — 96
Marking Corrections — 99
Typography — 102
Balloons — 107
Captions — 118

Appendix: Sample Style Sheet — 121
Glossary — 125
Resources — 131
Index — 137
About the Author — 142

INTRODUCTION

IN THIS CHAPTER:

What I Mean by "Comics"	8
Who This Book Is For	8
Notes on Terminology	11

I wrote *The Proofreader's Guide to Comic Book Style* for a simple reason: There wasn't an existing reference book for editorial style conventions and mechanics in North American comics. There are books about related parts of the comics creation and publishing process, many of which you can find listed in the **Resources**—like Shelly Bond's *Filth and Grammar* (which focuses on the developmental and art direction side of editing), Nate Piekos's *The Essential Guide to Comic Book Lettering* (a manual for the people actually doing the lettering), and Scott McCloud's beloved series on creating comics. And there are books on conventions in other formats and markets, like Jan Mitsuko Cash's *Editing Manga*. But I couldn't find one that focused on the nitty-gritty knowledge about "Western-style" comics I needed when I started working with them.

So I created it myself.

This guide doesn't pretend to be the universal authority on the right way to do things. There are few, if any, absolute rules in comics or any other type of publishing, and it would be impossible to create a guide that covers every conceivable situation. That said, I've done my best to document the ways writers, letterers, and publishers in this medium commonly handle important elements of editorial style, noting when one approach dominates and when preferences are all over the map. How closely any one comic follows the conventions here will vary widely depending on the tastes of the publisher or creator, the intended audience, whether it's a mainstream series or an experimental zine, and more.

Whatever your role in the comics world, I hope you find this handbook useful.

WHAT I MEAN BY "COMICS"

When I talk about comics throughout this book, I'm mainly talking about comics written and published in English for a North American audience—including comic books, graphic novels, comic strips, and webcomics. Although not everything in these categories follows exactly the same style, many of them share certain conventions.

Books published in other languages and for other markets have their own conventions, formats, and visual language. I'll be touching on a couple of the elements that come up in North American comics that are influenced by these styles, like manga, but my focus is Western-style publishing. The **Resources** include a couple of books that specifically cover manga style.

For more information on vocabulary, see **Notes on Terminology** at the end of this introduction and the **Glossary** at the end of the book. I'll get into what I mean by style in **chapter 2**.

WHO THIS BOOK IS FOR

I created this book with editors and proofreaders in mind—whether they already work in comics or they're new to the medium. But it can be a helpful reference for anyone who writes, letters, or publishes comics.

More specifically, *The Proofreader's Guide to Comic Book Style* focuses on the mechanics of copyediting and proofreading for comics scripts and lettered panels. It doesn't cover editing in the sense of acquiring and commissioning, developmental editing, or art direction—other books have already done that better than I could. But there are plenty of things in here that can be of use to editors who do that type of work, whether they're line editing or copyediting, reviewing the work of a proofreader, or updating a house style guide.

If you're a traditional publisher or self-publisher who doesn't have a style guide, this book will make the case for creating one, give you an idea of what you should include, and help you get the best work from your editorial freelancers.

Using This Book as an Editor or Proofreader

Although this book is, in part, a guide to proofreading and copyediting* comics, it assumes some amount of general editorial training or previous experience. Maybe you're a freelancer who's had general training as a copyeditor but never worked in comics. Maybe you're a commissioning editor of comics who wants to develop your proofreading skills. Maybe you're a managing editor updating your publisher's style guide. This work requires more than a stellar command of grammar and spelling—that's obviously a great place to start, but being familiar with style manuals and what sorts of rules they're likely to include is its own supplemental skill. You can find some information on both general and comics-specific editorial training in **Resources**.

Using This Book as a Writer

As a rule, writers in most media aren't expected to be experts in *The Chicago Manual of Style* or every arcane rule of grammar—that's part of why editors exist. And comics don't all follow a universal set of rules anyway.

But the more you know, the better you can serve yourself in the editorial process and the happier you'll make the person whose job it is to enforce the rules that *are* being followed. If you're working with a publisher, understanding common conventions and style guidelines in editing and proofreading can help you anticipate what changes might be made to your script and where you might need to advocate for yourself. If you're working with a freelance editor, it can help you be more deliberate about when you want to do things the way mainstream comics readers will expect and when you want to follow your own style.

As I'll get into in chapter 2, style is less about right and wrong than it is about consistency and expectations. Even in

---

* Copyediting often isn't a standalone step in comics publishing, but there are cases where it benefits everyone to include it. See **The Role(s) of the Editor** in chapter 1 and **The Case for Copyediting** in chapter 3.

the case of spelling or grammar, any rule can be broken with the right justification (and, if applicable, an editor who supports that justification). What's right in formal "standard" English isn't always right in a casual context or specific dialect. A good editor or proofreader will understand this, though even the best of us sometimes misstep. If a particular element of style or mechanics is important to you, bring it up early in the process so everyone involved can be aware of it.

Using This Book as a Publisher

As a publisher—whether you own or work for a big company or you're a self-publishing creator—the more complete your personal or company style guide (more on that in chapter 2), the better the editing and proofreading work you'll get, whether from in-house staff or from freelancers. Although there's always room to do things differently for a particular series or creator, having default rules and preferences documented in one place will help ensure everyone is working from the same starting point and create consistency across a publishing program. This book covers a variety of text-styling topics that either aren't mentioned in big guides like *The Chicago Manual of Style* or are usually handled differently in comics than they are in the types of prose publishing those guides cater to.

If you don't have someone on staff who's equipped to build your style guide, you can always hire an editor or editorial consultant like me to create one for you from scratch or update and improve an existing one.

There is a series of Publisher Tip sidebars throughout this book that feature advice specific to publishing companies and self-publishers.

NOTES ON TERMINOLOGY

Before I dive into the substance, I'd like to touch on a few terms that tend to be points of confusion or debate when it comes to talking about comics.

Comic or Graphic Novel?

The seemingly simple question "What's the difference between a comic and a graphic novel?" doesn't have a simple answer. Some people use *comics* as the umbrella term for all types of sequential art and *graphic novels* to refer to long-form storytelling under that umbrella (usually in contrast to comic books being stories told in individual issues). Others only call the short-form, episodic type comics and consider graphic novels a wholly separate thing. And some publishers call a collected edition of comics issues a graphic novel if they tell a single continuous story. Then there are other questions altogether, like whether "comics" includes single-panel works or manga.

Many writers have dived into this topic in much more detail, and I'm not the person to offer a definitive answer. But for the sake of simplicity, in this book, I'm using *comics* as a broad category term.

Digital Comic, Webcomic, or Webtoon?

The terminology is a bit squishy here, too, but it's worth talking about some of the distinctions that can be made among the different types of comics read on a screen.

Digital comics or *e-comics* usually refers to what are essentially digital versions of print comics, which can be published on either third-party or publisher-specific platforms. Although some of these are "digital first" (initially published in digital format and later followed by a print version) or even digital only, they tend to follow the format of a standard print issue or volume with pages. They generally read best on an e-reader or tablet.

Webcomics usually refers to comics that are made specifically for online publication on a website or app, don't necessarily follow the page format of a traditional print comic, and are released one episode, strip, or panel at a time. They're generally meant to be read on either a phone or a computer, though phones might have won out at this point. They might look similar to newspaper comic strips or, increasingly, use the vertical-scrolling *webtoon* format optimized for mobile reading. (Webtoon is also the name of the best-known platform that hosts and publishes webtoons.)

Digital comics can also be used as an umbrella term for all these formats.

In the US, comics from big traditional publishers more often fall into the first category, but not exclusively—Webtoon has published official comics by both DC and Marvel, for example. There are also cases that don't fit neatly into one category or the other, and some webcomics eventually end up in print.

Copyediting or Proofreading?

Although these terms mean distinct things to professional editors, a lot of people who don't do the work themselves aren't aware of the differences.

Copyediting is reviewing text for grammar and style, including punctuation, spelling, formatting, and consistency. It can also extend to things like word choice, sentence flow, and fact-checking. Generally, this work happens in Word or another word processing format and is done before it goes to a letterer or typesetter—though I cover some exceptions in **chapter 3**. That chapter gives a full rundown of the copyediting process for scripts and makes an argument for when and why copyediting can be beneficial.

Also, no book about copyediting would be complete without acknowledging that some people write "copyeditor" and some people write "copy editor." Neither one is right or wrong, and it's just a matter of style and preference.

Proofreading is reviewing materials—in comics, usually lettered panels and typeset text—for anything the editor or copyeditor (if there was one) might have missed as well as anything related to lettering and layout, including crossbar I's, word division, balloon errors, and more.

You might also hear the term *proof-edit*, especially in self-publishing spaces. This isn't a standardized term among professional editors and could refer to a final review of already copyedited text to catch any lingering errors before layout (either in addition to or instead of a proofread), a light copyedit that only looks for limited types of errors, or a heavy proofread of something that didn't get a copyedit.

I've tried to define other terms that might be unfamiliar over the course of this book. You can find them all collected in the **Glossary**.

1
EDITING, PROOFREADING, AND THE COMICS WORKFLOW

IN THIS CHAPTER:

Workflow Overview	16
The Role(s) of the Editor	21
The Role(s) of the Proofreader	27

It's helpful for anyone who's part of the publishing process to understand how their work fits into the overall creation of the finished product.

Besides the editing and proofreading roles I'll be discussing in more detail in the rest of this chapter, here are some of the key creative roles that may be involved in the publishing process.

- writer: the person who comes up with the story concept and worldbuilding and/or writes the script (the same person or team very often does both, but not always)
- penciller: the first person who interprets the script into artwork
- inker: the person who uses the pencils as a guide to create the final line art
- colorist: the person who applies color to the line art (in the case of a grayscale comic, the inker might do everything, or the artwork might go to another artist for tones)
- flatter: someone who assists the colorist by mapping out the colorable areas in a digital file
- letterer: the person who places the dialogue, captions, some or all sound effects, and other text in the comic and creates the balloons, boxes, and other shapes that contain it
- cover artist(s): the person or people who create the cover of a comic, who might be a different person or team from the penciller, inker, and colorist who create the interior
- designer: the person who creates design elements that aren't part of the comic itself—for example, the jacket and front and back matter of a printed book
- production (or prepress) artist: the person who combines and prepares the artwork and lettering for print or digital publication, which may include implementing art and proofreading corrections

In both traditionally published and self-published comics, two or more of these roles might be filled by the same person or team. In particular, among pencilling, inking, and coloring, two or more roles might be combined with each other—if you see a single "art by" credit, that's generally what it means. An artist might letter their own work, and some or all of the production work might be done by the letterer or designer.

Writers, pencillers, inkers, colorists, and cover artists all fall under the umbrella of comics creators. Some creators who write, illustrate, and letter their own comics also call themselves cartoonists, but usage varies depending on the type of work and individual preference.

WORKFLOW OVERVIEW

What follows is an example of a possible comics workflow at a traditional publisher. This won't be the exact process at all publishers, especially self-publishing creators, but many of the steps will be similar.

This chart is based on a workflow in which the writer, penciller, inker, colorist, and letterer are all different people, but as noted in the introduction to this chapter, two or more of these roles are sometimes combined. It also doesn't include anything that happens before the script is written (like the idea development that may happen between the writer and editor) or after the comic is finalized for distribution.

A writer might or might not see copyediting changes before the script moves to the next step in the process. This will depend on the publisher's practices, the number and nature of the changes, and whether the copyeditor has any questions that can only be answered by the writer. However, unless the writer is working in a very limited capacity, they will see the art and lettering.

The letterer and proofreader might not initially receive the complete colored artwork—if the schedule demands it, the editor might send them the black-and-white inks. In these cases, the letterer might eventually get the colors, but the proofreader might not. (For more, see **How Are Comics Proofread?** later in this chapter.) If the letterer doesn't see the final colors, a production artist may have to adjust the colors used in the lettering to make sure everything goes together. As noted at the beginning of this chapter, the production artist might also be the one to implement other final changes in place of an artist or letterer doing it themselves.

When a comic's inks, colors, and letters are created by three different people, they are generally three separate layers that can be stacked on top of one another in one file—so although they are listed as separate elements in the flow chart, they will be combined when they go to the proofreader or writer. I haven't shown the step of creating this combined file, but it will generally be done by the same person who preps everything for production.

Microsoft Word is the most common default program for scripts. On the art and design side, Adobe's suite of apps is an industry standard among print publishers, so Photoshop, Illustrator, InDesign, and Acrobat are common for art, lettering, layout/production, and proofreading, respectively. For webcomics, Clip Studio Paint and Procreate are also popular.

Comics that are originally published in another language (like Japanese manga and French bandes dessinées) and translated for an English-speaking audience can bring their own special workflow considerations. For example, it's common for an English-language publisher to be beholden to the size and shape of balloons and caption boxes from the original and only able to replace the text itself. Sound effects outside balloons and other text that is part of the artwork might or might not be translated.

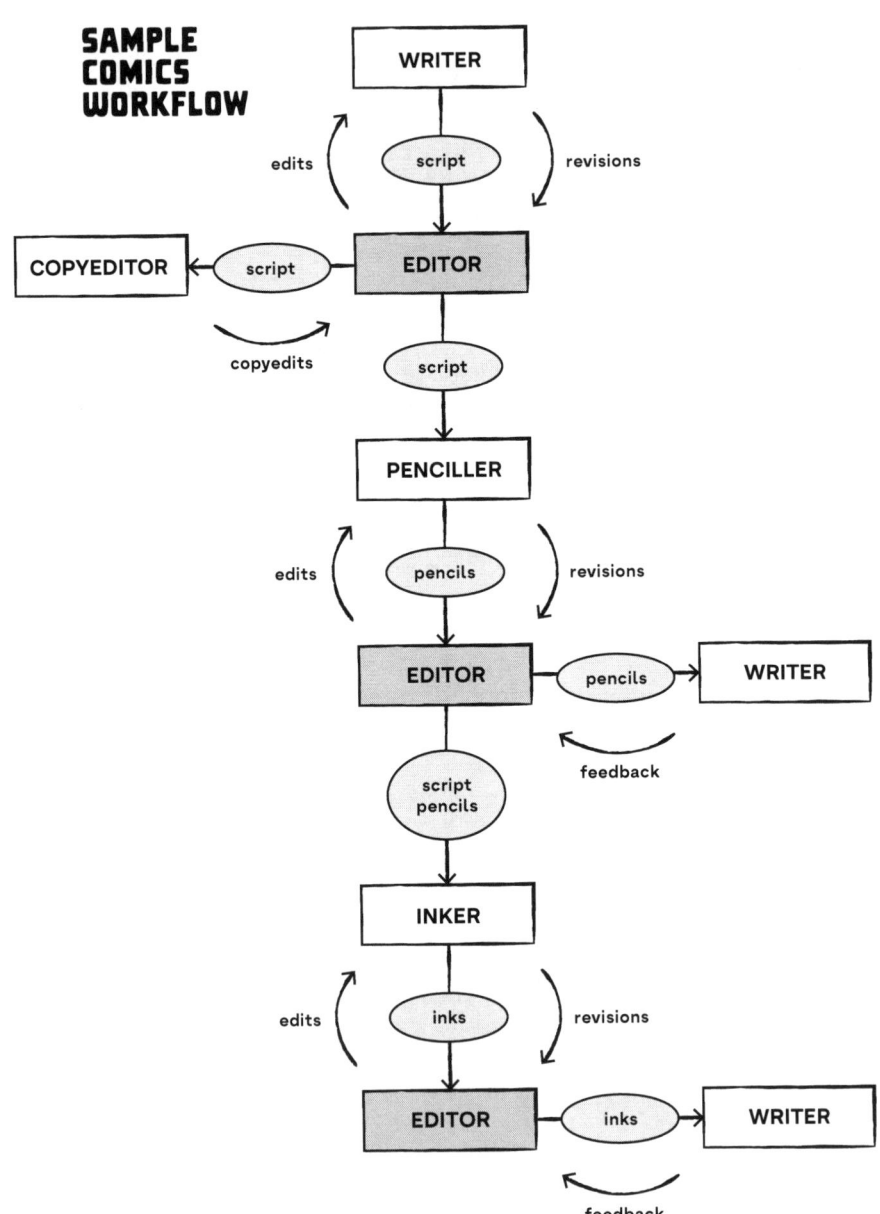

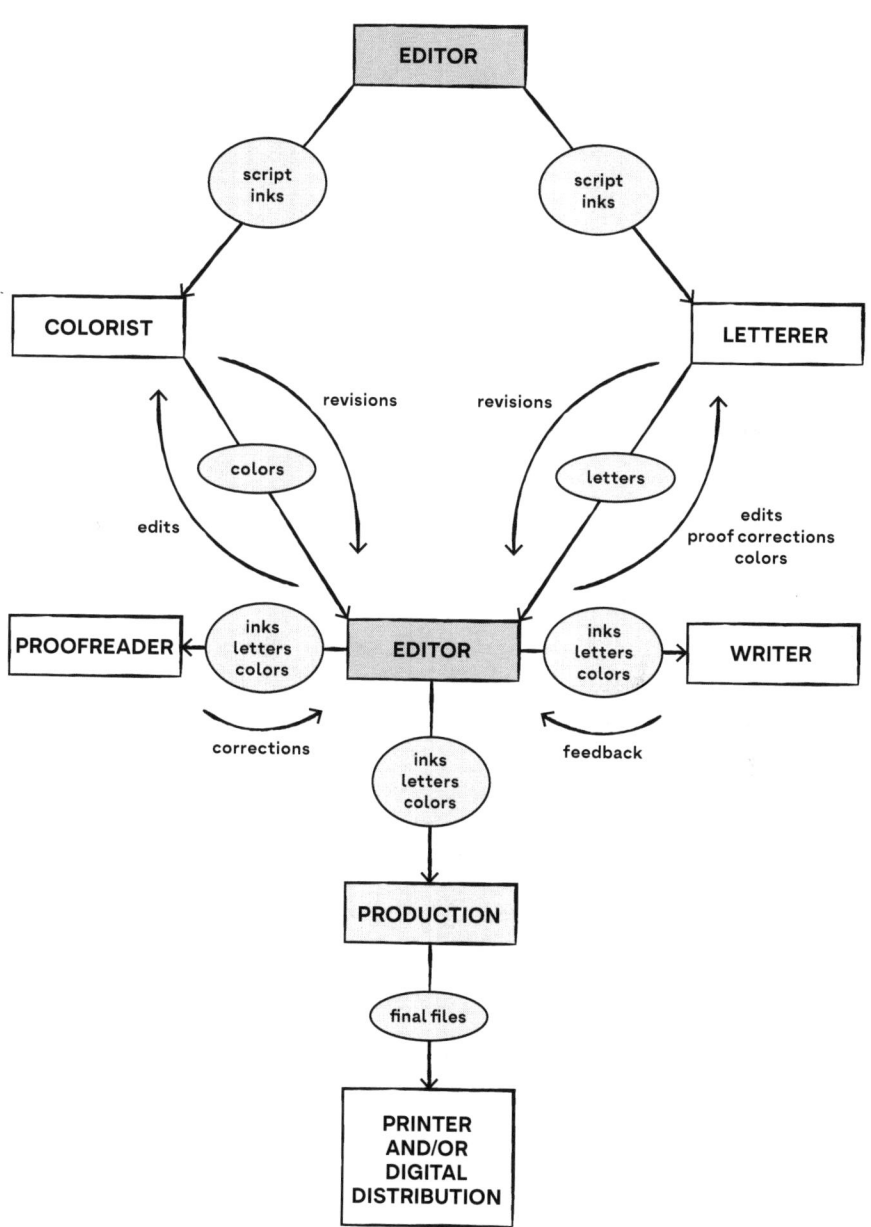

COMICS VS. PROSE

If you come from the world of prose book publishing, be aware that the editorial and production process works differently in comics. This is especially true at comics-specific publishers, as opposed to companies that publish both prose books and sequential stories.

Here are some of the differences to expect.

- **Editing:** In prose, *editor* is a general term that could refer to an acquiring or commissioning editor, a production editor, or a copyeditor. In comics, *editor* by itself is a specific title whose closest analog to prose is acquiring or commissioning editor, but the correspondence isn't one-to-one.

- **Copyediting:** Prose books put out by reputable publishers generally go through a dedicated copyedit phase, but many comics don't. When that's the case, the work is divvied up between the editor and the proofreader.

- **Proofreading:** It's rare for prose book publishers to have in-house proofreaders these days, but some large comics publishers have one or more on staff.

- **Design:** Prose books and magazines are typeset and designed; comics are lettered and illustrated, except for limited elements like copyright pages and introductory essays.

- **Publishing timelines:** Although the time from script submission to final publication might not be wildly different for a graphic novel than it is for a prose book, turnaround times are (unsurprisingly) much shorter for periodicals.

THE ROLE(S) OF THE EDITOR

Editor

The comics editor is a broad role that encompasses many aspects of the comics creation process. When an editor is working in-house for a publisher, their responsibilities might include reviewing submissions and choosing what to acquire; developing their own concepts and hiring creators to execute them; pitching books to a publisher's editorial board to get approval; negotiating contracts with creators; serving as developmental editor and art director in collaboration with the creators; hiring and reviewing the work of copyeditors, proofreaders, and other editorial freelancers; ensuring files are properly transmitted to the production team; and more. When an editor is working as a freelancer with a self-publishing creator or small press, they might be more narrowly focused on the developmental editing and art direction aspects or include heavier production-related work.

When a comic doesn't get a dedicated copyedit, the work that a copyeditor would do is effectively shared between the editor and the proofreader. How much falls to each person might be driven by their respective strengths and weaknesses or the preferences of the publisher. However, one great practice in these situations is for the editor to start a style sheet—the summary of spelling, punctuation, formatting, and other style preferences for the project. No matter how thorough a publisher's style guide is, it's rare not to have any decisions to make or proper nouns to document for an individual book, and having at least some of those decisions resolved before lettering saves time and effort for the proofreader, the editor, and the letterer. (For an overview of style sheets, style guides, and style manuals, see **chapter 2**. For a sample style sheet, see the **appendix**.)

An editor might be supported by an editorial assistant, associate editor, or assistant editor—who might do anything from administrative work to editing their own books—or they might have none of those.

Copyeditor

The main job of a copyeditor is reviewing written text for grammar and style, including punctuation, capitalization, spelling, formatting, and consistency. (I go into more detail about what *style* encompasses in **chapter 2**.) As part of this work, they should create a style sheet for each project, or update an existing one if one already exists—again, see chapter 2. Copyediting could also include checking for continuity errors, improving sentence flow, checking factual references or anachronisms, or suggesting changes related to inclusive language (see page 25).

Comics often don't go through a dedicated copyediting step, and the reasons for this vary. Sometimes the word count is small enough that the editor or publisher doesn't feel like it's worth it. Sometimes the schedule makes it difficult or downright impossible (especially for a monthly or biweekly series). Sometimes significant edits will be happening at the lettering stage for fit or other reasons, so it doesn't make sense to copyedit beforehand. Sometimes the editor is a really strong copyeditor. And sometimes it boils down to "This is how it's always been done."

Although in many cases copyediting really is either unnecessary or impractical, there are many other cases where it can benefit the work and everyone involved—see **The Case for Copyediting** in chapter 3.

When a standalone copyediting pass does happen in comics, it happens at the script stage, unless there isn't a script. Usually, only the text that will be lettered, like dialogue and captions, is copyedited. But a publisher might choose to copyedit the whole script, including things like stage directions, sometimes in anticipation of it being published on its own at some point or adapted into an audio version. Most often, this is done in Microsoft Word using Track Changes.

Ideally, copyediting should be the very last thing done to the script before it goes to the letterer. For example, if at all possible, any tweaks the writer or editor might decide to make to the script once they see the artwork should be incorporated before the copyeditor sees it. This is both a matter of respect for the letterer or production artist, who will have to implement any changes identified during proofreading, and the best way to ensure an error-free finished product. The more errors there are for a proofreader to mark, the higher the chances that they'll miss one—or that a new error will be introduced in the process of implementing those corrections. Freelance lettering services also usually only include a certain number of corrections as part of the base rate. If there are more, the publisher will have to pay extra or do the work in-house.

Chapter 3 covers the specifics of scope, format, and process for copyediting scripts.

Other Types of Editors

Here are a few other editorial roles you might see in comics publishing. Not every publisher will have all of these, and terminology varies.

Managing Editor

A managing editor is, in many ways, the air traffic controller of a publishing company, imprint, or team. They track everything being published, ensure proper handoff between departments, and keep titles on schedule. They might also be responsible for hiring and overseeing editorial freelancers. Even if a publisher doesn't have a dedicated role called "managing editor," there will usually be a person who fulfills these responsibilities. The position might be called something else, or the duties might be folded into another position—like production coordinator, prepress manager, or head of proofreading. (Conversely, there's sometimes a role called managing editor that encompasses different responsibilities.)

Production Editor

Like a managing editor, a production editor (or editorial project manager) tracks books as they move through the process and ensures all the people involved have what they need. Where the managing editor generally focuses on the entire title list for a publisher or imprint, a production editor generally focuses on a more limited number of individual books or series. An assistant editor or editorial assistant does this work at some companies.

Editor in Chief
The editor in chief is usually responsible for the overall editorial direction of a publisher or imprint. They also play a role in business operations. The editor in chief sometimes acquires and edits individual titles (more common at smaller publishers) and sometimes doesn't.

Localization Editor
A localization editor reads text that has been translated from another language to ensure it reads naturally for its intended audience while preserving any important cultural context.

Subject Matter Expert or Content Reviewer
These terms refer to someone who reads for factual accuracy related to something like a profession, hobby, scientific field, or language.

Authenticity or Sensitivity Reader
If a comic features a character with a background different from the writer's, it can be helpful to hire someone to make sure the story feels believable. This is where an authenticity reader or sensitivity reader can provide valuable feedback. Some people use these terms interchangeably. Others use *authenticity reader* to refer to someone who checks that the experiences or behavior of a character feels realistic based on their background or identity and *sensitivity reader* for someone who identifies any language, plot points, or characterization related to marginalized groups that readers might find outdated or hurtful, whether any of the characters belong to those groups or not. (Many general copyeditors and proofreaders also comment on some of these aspects, usually collectively referred to as conscious language or inclusive language, as part of their work.)

COMICS AND CONSCIOUS LANGUAGE

Conscious language, or inclusive language, is a type of writing and editing that aims to avoid both overt and implicit bias as well as anything that could alienate readers of a particular race, culture, gender, sexuality, disability, or other identity. This can involve anything from the choice of a single word to the overall characterization and plot development of a story.

In a form like comics, where space is limited and the language is often casual, irreverent, or funny, well-meaning creators might worry that incorporating conscious language will make their writing stilted or wordy or that it will kill their jokes. But just like overall editorial style, it isn't about making everyone follow a rigid approach to writing with tons of specific rules. It's just about being mindful of your characterization and word choice to avoid unintentionally hurting or excluding people.

If you do it right, most readers will never notice that you've done anything to be inclusive—but people *will* notice hurtful or exclusionary language, even if it's not used on purpose. And why give a potential fan a reason to stop reading?

There are whole books dedicated to inclusive language, and I've listed some of them in the **Resources**.

ACCESSIBILITY IN COMICS

To make sure a comic can be read by as many people as possible, it's important to think about accessibility early in the publishing process.

Although comics are a visual medium, there are multiple ways to make them accessible to blind and low-vision readers. Matthew Shifrin, the creator of Bricks for the Blind, has written about how life-changing it was when he discovered a way to access the comics he grew up hearing about but never being able to read. Accessibility options include audio descriptive versions (either fully produced like an audiobook or audio play or published as text intended for use with a screen reader), braille, and tactile printed shapes. The Accessible Comics for the Blind Project has highlighted some creative solutions.

There are other types of accessibility to think about in comics as well. For example, publishers should consider how their comics will appear to color-blind readers and what fonts will be harder or easier for readers with dyslexia and other processing differences to parse. While not every comic will be equally accessible to every reader, small changes can hugely affect who can enjoy them.

Different solutions will involve different editing processes, and not every editor or copyeditor will be experienced with those processes. In addition to making sure text is formatted and styled the way your production team needs, they may need to do things like capitalizing hashtags and URLs in a way that lets screen readers parse them correctly.

THE ROLE(S) OF THE PROOFREADER

At some point after a comic has been lettered—ideally when everything is close to final—it goes to the proofreader for review.

As mentioned in the editor section of this chapter, if a comic doesn't go through a dedicated copyedit, the proofreader might handle some of the work that a copyeditor would otherwise do. For example, they could be encouraged to mark not just outright errors but suggestions for improving sentence flow, word choice, and other elements that would be considered overstep for a proofreader in other types of publishing.

Whenever possible, a book should go to the proofreader after the editor and writer have already reviewed the lettering rather than at the same time (or before). Otherwise, an error could be introduced through a revision—whether because the new text the editor sends to the letterer inadvertently goes against house style (or even contains a typo) or because the letterer unknowingly introduces an extra character when pasting it into their design program—and the proofreader would never have the opportunity to catch it.

How Are Comics Proofread?

How a proofreader reviews a comic will depend on what type of comic it is.

Comics designed for either print or print-style digital publication are most often proofread as PDFs,[*] whether through downloaded files or in the cloud. Because the files can get huge, it's common for the proofreader to receive a downsized version, which is easier to work with but can sometimes make it difficult to confirm suspected errors or even difficult to read if the resolution is too low. For this reason, it's helpful to have a file with low-res artwork but sharp lettering. Other options include web-based review systems and, for digital comics, epub files.

---

[*] Some publishers still have their proofreaders work on hard copy, but it's less and less common. The pandemic eliminated the practice at a lot of the remaining holdouts.

Some webcomics also use PDFs for review, but proofreaders might instead be viewing image files or reading on a dedicated publishing platform.

Proofreaders who have experience with PDFs know there are a variety of display quirks in Acrobat and other viewers that can cause you to think there's an error when there isn't (or that there isn't one when there is). These include but aren't limited to line weights not displaying properly, entire elements not showing up at certain magnifications, and fonts looking weird. When in doubt, query.

The standard form of proofreading is a "cold read" of the lettered panels, but another type of review is the comparison read, where the proofreader is checking the comic either against the final script—to make sure everything that was supposed to be lettered has been lettered, all special styling has been applied correctly, and no errors have been introduced in the lettering process—or against a previous round of corrections—to make sure they've all been incorporated.

Depending on the publisher or the individual book, it's possible that the proofreader will review not a completed comic but lettering over uncolored inks (or even, in some cases, pencils). This isn't ideal, since it can lead to the proofreader missing an error that relates to the art, but it's sometimes the way things have to work on a rush project.

See **chapter 4** for more on proofreading scope, how comics are marked up, and common typography and balloon errors to watch for.

WORKING WITH COPYEDITORS AND PROOFREADERS

When you send a project to a copyeditor or proofreader, they'll need your in-house style guide or, at minimum, instructions on which style manual and which dictionary they should follow (for example, *The Chicago Manual of Style* and *Merriam-Webster's Collegiate Dictionary*). If you don't have a style guide, it's important to know how general style manuals tend to differ from common comics conventions. I talk a lot about that in **chapter 2**, and it's a big reason why you should put a style guide together—even if it's just a single page of exceptions. If you have a style sheet for the project, include that as well.

Your proofreader will also need to know how you want them to mark their corrections—see **Marking Corrections** in chapter 4.

2

EDITORIAL STYLE

IN THIS CHAPTER:

What Is Style?	31
How to Use This Chapter	34
Capitalization	35
Punctuation	40
Numbers	54
Formatting	57
Captions, Notes, and Bursts	65
Special Symbols	69
Spelling	72

WHAT IS STYLE?

Editorial style is, in a nutshell, everything having to do with how text is formatted. It includes capitalization, punctuation, spelling, typography, lettering, and things like when to use italics and whether to write "21" or "twenty-one." It can also include grammar and word usage.

Style guidelines are meant to help you be clear and consistent, not declare what's objectively right or wrong. Each publisher or creator will have their own style preferences, whether that's writing a comic in all lowercase or wanting to treat a single punctuation mark in a special way. And whatever style they follow, they'll occasionally ignore a given rule for the sake of voice or readability. Despite sometimes being stereotyped as humorless sticklers, good copyeditors and proofreaders understand the balance of when to change something and when to leave it alone even if it's "wrong."

In other words, it's not just a matter of learning rules and applying them—there's judgment in knowing which rule to apply and when not to apply a rule at all. Like law or medicine, editorial work is both an art and a science. (Thankfully, the stakes are usually a bit lower for us.)

Style References

Style guide is often used as a catchall term. To keep things clear, for the purposes of this book, I'll be distinguishing between *style manuals*, *style guides*, and *style sheets* using the definitions that follow, but it's very common to hear "style guide" used for any or all of these.

Style manual: A published reference book that lays out style and grammar guidelines. Again, the primary purpose of a style manual isn't to decide what's universally right and wrong but to help publishers make their content consistent. For example, it's not objectively right or wrong to use the serial ("Oxford") comma—the one that comes before the "and" in "Lions, tigers, and bears"—but you generally want to be consistent about whether and when you use it throughout a book.

Widely used US style manuals include *The Chicago Manual of Style* and the stylebooks of the Associated Press (AP), American Psychological Association (APA), American Medical Association (AMA), and Modern Language Association (MLA). *Chicago* is the most common choice among general-audience ("trade") publishers, especially for fiction, and many comics publishers use it as their default. But space is at a premium in comics, and some publishers prefer AP, which is designed for newspapers and magazines—types of publishing with similar constraints.

Style guide: A document that lays out the preferred style for a specific company, imprint, property, or creator. It generally indicates which style manual and which dictionary the publisher follows, along with any other references, and then lists the style rules that either aren't covered by or depart from those references. For example, a publisher might mostly follow *The Chicago Manual of Style* but apply different rules for when to use numerals and when to spell out a number. The style guide can also document practices for how things like indicia, credits, tables of contents, and captions should be formatted, and some publishers include their guidance for letterers as part of the editorial style guide.

The preferences and guidelines documented in a style guide (or the chosen style manual and dictionary, if a publisher doesn't have its own dedicated style guide) are often referred to as the publisher's "house style."

Style sheet: A document created for a single book or series. This builds on a style manual or style guide, highlighting important points specific to an individual work and, as with the style guide, any exceptions. This could include the correct spelling for character names, other proper nouns, and any in-universe invented words; punctuation or style decisions for certain types of captions; whether the writer prefers "y'know" or "ya know"; or whether a comma is used before "too" at the end of a sentence.

In addition, a style sheet might include key details about settings and characters, like distances, in-world mechanics, and ages. Depending on how much of this sort of information there is to document, it might be spun off into one or more separate documents, often called character bibles or story bibles.

See the **appendix** for a sample style sheet.

BUILDING A STYLE GUIDE

A style guide is an essential tool for any publisher—big company or solo self-publishing creator—to maintain correctness and consistency across everything you publish and to get the best work from editors and proofreaders. Sending a freelance proofreader a clear and comprehensive style guide will both help them do things the way you want and save you both a lot of time on questions.

This document can be as short as a page or as long as fifty pages. Somewhere in between is usually the most helpful—long enough to cover all the bases and not so long that people might not read the whole thing—but it'll come down to how much information you need to document, including whether you want to fully spell out rules from your chosen style manual or only include things that can't be found there.

You can build your style guide yourself or hire someone like me to do it for you. If you build it yourself and don't have an experienced copyeditor or proofreader on staff, it's a good idea to have someone who is look it over and make sure everything is clear and nothing important is missing.

HOW TO USE THIS CHAPTER

This book is meant to supplement your or your client's style manual of choice, which will have in-depth guidance on a variety of specific situations. The information here isn't intended to be exhaustive on its own but rather to highlight common conventions and preferences that copyeditors and proofreaders of comics should be aware of, especially when they differ from other types of publishing.

This is also not a guide to grammar, story editing, or the craft of writing. For some helpful books on those topics, see **Resources**.

Some of the elements I cover in this chapter are unique to comics. Others have special considerations in this medium or just tend to be a little idiosyncratic in comics compared to other types of publishing. I've also included a few points that are common to most types of publishing but that often trip up writers and editors.

The conventions laid out here are based on North American comics and graphic novel publishing. Comics published in other countries, and translations of those comics published for the US or Canadian market, might follow different styles.

There isn't one single way to do things, and you'll see words like "might," "often," and "generally" a lot, but I'll indicate where one style dominates and where I recommend one choice over others as best practice. Works like webcomics, independent or experimental comics, and literary graphic novels are more likely to break widespread convention than traditionally published print comics—or, especially in the case of comics influenced by overseas formats, to follow conventions that are more common outside North America.

CAPITALIZATION

The Crossbar I	36
Drop Caps	37
Hashtags, URLs, and Usernames	37
Personal Titles, Ranks, and Kinship Names	37
Proper Nouns and "The"	38
Punctuation and Capitalization	39
Small Caps	39
Title Case	39

Comics have traditionally used all-caps text. Among other benefits, this means you don't have to worry about letter ascenders and descenders and can fit lines of text closer together.

You might be more likely to see mixed-case text in comics that are self-published, published by a small press, or intended for young readers, but there are plenty of big-name publishers and adult comics that use this style as well. Also, even if a comic uses all-caps text overall, it might use other capitalization styles in certain contexts, like mixed case when a character is muttering or whispering, lowercase text for hesitation sounds or text within breath marks, or aLtErNaTiNg CaPs when a character is being sarcastic or losing consciousness. You might also see different styles used for different characters. On the flip side, if a comic uses mixed case overall, it might occasionally use all caps for emphasis or shouting.

Regardless of the lettering style, text shouldn't be written in all caps at the script stage—the script should use mixed case, and the letterer will set it in all caps if applicable. Among other things, this sets the text up correctly for crossbar I's. However, comics scripts do often use all caps for some of the text that isn't meant to be lettered, like character names (especially when indicating who's speaking), much like TV and movie scripts do. For more on script formatting, see **chapter 3**.

If a comic is in all caps, you won't have to worry about some of the things covered in this section, like when to capitalize "Mom" or the first word after an ellipsis. On the other hand, the use of small caps will matter more than it would in mixed case. Capitalization style also influences other conventions and styling decisions, like whether to use periods in acronyms.

The Crossbar I

It's a standard convention that in comics lettering, the capital letter *I* is a plain vertical line (often called a slash I) in most placements, but when it's used for the pronoun *I*—including "I'd," "I'll," and any other contraction—you'll see horizontal bars at the top and bottom (the crossbar I or barred I). Depending on the publisher, comic, or letterer, the crossbar I may be used for other specific cases that should be listed in the style guide or style sheet, like Roman numerals, acronyms, the first letter in a proper noun, or the first word in a sentence. When a comic uses the crossbar I, one of the proofreader's responsibilities is making sure it's applied correctly.

HOW IS IT ALMOST NOON? I'M LATE!

This practice was born in an era when print quality for comics wasn't great and a single plain line risked disappearing on the page. This isn't as much of an issue these days (especially in digital comics), and some modern letterers and publishers will choose to use the slash I for everything. On the other hand, using the crossbar I for everything isn't considered good practice.

In most all-caps lettering fonts, typing a lowercase *i* will get you the slash I and typing a capital *I* will get you the crossbar. This is one reason scripts should be written in mixed case even if the text will be lettered in all caps—it makes for one less thing the letterer will have to do manually, which means both less work for them and fewer opportunities for errors to be introduced. (Again, see **chapter 3** for script formatting.)

Drop Caps

Although less common than it used to be, a drop cap (dropped capital) or other type of decorative letter is sometimes used in elements like captions. It's important to make sure this is applied consistently—both whether and when the special cap is used and how it's styled, including the typeface, size, and color.

> **O**nce upon a midnight dreary, while I pondered, weak and weary...

Hashtags, URLs, and Usernames

For any multiword hashtag, website, or username that might be read using a screen reader by blind or low-vision users, it's best to use Pascal case (#LikeThis) rather than all lowercase (#likethis) to make sure the words are parsed correctly.

This can be helpful for sighted readers too. If one of these elements will be set in all caps or all lowercase, it's worth thinking about any possible misreadings.

Personal Titles, Ranks, and Kinship Names

Whether and when to capitalize formal titles, familial words, and other words that might come before a person's name will depend on the style manual and/or style guide. That said, the usual style in US publishing is to capitalize them when they're part of the name (President Jane Doe, Uncle Joe) but not otherwise (the president, her uncle Joe). Kinship terms that completely replace a name are usually capitalized ("He's my dad" but "I told Dad I'm not going").

Words in all these categories are also usually capitalized in direct address: "Hi, Mom"; "What's wrong with me, Doctor?"; "Put me in, Coach." On the other hand, terms of endearment like "dear" and "sweetie" and informal titles or positions usually aren't capitalized when used by themselves in direct address. Terms of address like "sir" are usually lowercase in general use ("Excuse me, sir") but have distinctive capitalization conventions in certain adult genres and subcultures.

Proper Nouns and "The"

If you're working with mixed-case text, the question of whether and when to capitalize "the" before a proper noun—like the name of a place, group, or character—will come up sooner or later. Under standard *Chicago* style, a midsentence "the" is virtually never capitalized,* and you'd write "the Flash," "the Avengers," "the White House," etc. by default. The AP, on the other hand, capitalizes the "The" if it's part of a company's formal name.

But besides the fact that some comics creators and publishers feel strongly that "the" should be capitalized if it's part of a name, an in-house lawyer might insist on it for trademark enforcement reasons. The trademark capitalization might apply in all circumstances or just some. (For more, see **Brands** in the Spelling section.) There might also be an exception for "ironic" caps, like when someone is just The Absolute Worst.

---

* Practically the only official exception to this is The Hague. *Chicago* does recognize that there's always room for publisher discretion. But the manual's editors don't recommend capitalizing the article in a name like the Ohio State University, and that school really, *really* wants you to capitalize it.

Punctuation and Capitalization

Colons
Whether the first word after a colon is capitalized will depend on the style guide and style manual. *The Chicago Manual of Style* used to only capitalize if the colon introduced two or more complete sentences, but as of the 18th edition, both *Chicago* and AP now capitalize if it introduces one or more complete sentences.

Dashes and Hyphens
When dashes or hyphens are used to indicate stammering or stuttering, the successive instances of the repeated sound are generally capitalized only if it's the first letter of a proper noun ("Wh-what are y-you?" but "N-New York"). For more information on this mechanic, see **Repeated Sounds** on page 46.

Ellipses
When an ellipsis is used at the beginning of a sentence and the lettering uses mixed case, some publishers and creators capitalize the first word and others don't.

Small Caps
For readability, a comic set in all caps might use small caps (or lowercase letters) in names with internal capitalization as well as possessives and plurals of acronyms, initialisms, numbers, or single capital letters. For more on names, see **Spelling**.

MACDONALD
SENTIENT A.I.S
THE 1800S

MacDONALD
SENTIENT A.I.s
THE 1800s

Title Case
Style manuals and individual publishers vary on how to capitalize the overall title of a book or series and any other works mentioned within a comic.

Some comics publishers follow the standard conventions of whichever style manual they use as their primary reference, but it's not uncommon to use a hybrid style—for example, mostly following *Chicago* but capitalizing all prepositions of four letters or more like AP does. (Until recently, *Chicago* lowercased all prepositions in titles no matter the length, but as of the 18th edition, it capitalizes them if they're five letters or longer.)

Elements like chapter titles and time and place captions might be capitalized the same way as titles of works, or they might use sentence case. You might also see all lowercase as a design choice.

For italics and quotation marks with titles, see **Formatting**.

PUNCTUATION

Ampersands	41
Apostrophes	41
Asterisks	42
Brackets	42
Colons	42
Commas	42
Dashes and Hyphens	44
Ellipses	47
Exclamation Points	48
Periods	49
Punctuation and Dialogue	49
Question Marks	50
Quotation Marks	50
Combined Punctuation	52

Because comics usually have relatively small word counts but a high proportion of dialogue, punctuation tends to stand out and may be used in "nonstandard" ways. Although there are general rules and conventions, communicating the right tone or meaning to the reader often takes precedence over "correctness."

One thing that sets comics apart from other types of publishing is that punctuation usually uses the style of the text that precedes it if there isn't a space in between—so an exclamation point that follows a phrase set in bold italics for emphasis will likewise be set in bold italics even if the punctuation isn't "part of" that emphasized phrase. See **Emphasis** in the Formatting section for a full explanation of this convention, especially as it relates to paired and successive punctuation marks.

Ampersands

Ampersands are most likely to show up in titles and other display type, where they're often a design choice, and credits, where a publisher might have different rules for the use of "and" versus "&" depending on whether two creators are working as a team. Elsewhere, spelling out "and" is the norm, though company names might be an exception.

Apostrophes

Apostrophe errors abound and can be sneaky, especially since they're hard to spot in some lettering fonts. Abbreviated words are common in dialogue, and it's not unusual for the apostrophe (') at the start of a word to be "backward"—i.e., an improperly used opening single quotation mark (').

Incorrect:	Correct:
IN THE '80s	**IN THE '80s**
'SCUSE ME!	**'SCUSE ME!**

It's also important to watch for straight apostrophes. Directional (curly, or "smart") apostrophes should usually be used unless house style calls for straight ones or a deliberate exception is being made for a specific comic or creator. Above all, the usage should be consistent—you don't want a haphazard mix of curly and straight.

See **Possessives and Plurals** under Formatting for the use of apostrophes in those contexts.

Asterisks

When footnotes appear in a comic, they're most often marked with asterisks. The asterisk that refers to the note generally does not have a space before it; it might be superscript, but very often it's regular text. The asterisk that begins the note itself might or might not be followed by a space depending on publisher preference, but it should not be superscript.

For the placement of reference asterisks relative to other punctuation, see **Combined Punctuation**. For more information on footnotes, see **Notes** under Captions, Notes, and Bursts and **Languages Other Than English** under Formatting.

Another use of asterisks is in place of breath marks (whiskers) to indicate sounds—see **Breath Marks** under Special Symbols.

Brackets

Angle brackets may be used to indicate text "translated" from another language (see **Languages Other Than English**). A variety of bracket types may be used in scripts to indicate text that will be set in breath marks (see **Breath Marks**).

Colons

Whether the first word after a colon is capitalized will depend on the style guide and style manual. *The Chicago Manual of Style* used to only capitalize if the colon introduced two or more complete sentences, but as of the 18th edition, both *Chicago* and AP now capitalize if it introduces one or more complete sentences.

Commas

Comics writers often have wide latitude when it comes to comma use, especially in speech, though some publishers are more prescriptive and lay out specific rules in their style guides (see the Considering Commas sidebar on the next page). As with anything in copyediting and proofreading, consistency is usually the most important thing.

CONSIDERING COMMAS

Comma use can vary a lot among writers and publishers. When sending a book to a copyeditor or proofreader, it's helpful for them to know how much they should defer to the writer versus your chosen style manual.

Types of commas whose use (or not) is usually dictated by the style manual or style guide include:

- serial comma, a.k.a. Oxford comma ("Lions, tigers, and bears")
- comma before Jr. and Sr. in names
- comma with direct address ("Hi, Mom!"; "Stay there, kid")
- appositive commas with dates and locations ("The Los Angeles, California, publisher")

Types of commas that are often specified in a style guide or variable from book to book:

- comma after a word like "oh," "so," or "well"
- comma after an introductory phrase like "Last year"
- comma before a sentence or phrase ender like "all right?," "huh?," "okay?," "though," or "too"
- commas with "like" when it's used as an approximator ("It was like 100 degrees out!") or pause filler ("It's, like, really confusing")
- comma before "a.k.a."
- comma before a conjunction that joins two independent clauses ("She waited all day, but he never showed up")
- comma splice—when just a comma joins two independent clauses ("I don't want to go inside, that house looks creepy")

Dashes and Hyphens

Most US style manuals use the em dash for a midsentence break or interrupted speech ("It's better than bad—it's good!"). Some use the en dash, which is shorter than the em but longer than a hyphen, for number ranges ("issues #42–#47"), joining open compounds ("post–World War II"), and other functions. A comic book may use neither, both, or just one of these.

Em Dashes and Double Dashes

The traditional style in comics is to use two hyphens (--), often called a double dash,* in place of a solid em dash (—). Why? The short answer is that's the way it's been done for decades.

For a longer answer, I'll defer to letterer Todd Klein, who has written about this topic on his blog: "When comics got to the point where scripts were typed out on a typewriter for someone to copy when lettering, the usual way to indicate an em-dash was a double dash, since there was no em-dash symbol on a typewriter. Typesetters and printers knew to convert the double dash to an em-dash when a typewritten script was copied into set type, but letterers probably didn't know or follow that convention, and the double dash gradually became the common form."

You can expect to see the double dash more often than not in mainstream Western comics. Some of the contexts where you might be more likely to see em dashes include comics that use mixed-case lettering; that are influenced by manga, manhua, and manhwa (Japanese, Chinese, and Korean comics); and that are published either independently by a creator or by a publisher that primarily focuses on prose.

Also, it's common for publishers to use solid em dashes in typeset elements that aren't part of the lettered comic, like indicia, back cover copy, and other marketing text.

---

* It's true that *double dash* isn't exactly an accurate term—hyphens and dashes are different things. But it's what people commonly call it, so it's what I've used in this book. I almost never hear *double hyphen* in the wild.

The solid em dashes available in many lettering fonts are on the shorter side. Decisions about dash style are ultimately between the letterer and the editor, but if the dashes feel awkwardly or confusingly short, it's worth the proofreader mentioning that as a global note.

Spacing with Dashes
Usually, there are no spaces around an em dash or double dash except in something like an editor's note or marketing blurb, where there's most often a space between the main text and the dash that introduces the attribution.

NO--DON'T GO!
*SEE ISSUE #79! --M.V.

Interruptions
As in prose writing, a dash at the end of a line of dialogue indicates speech being cut off suddenly, as with another character interrupting them or the speaker breaking off on their own accord (unless it's a bridging dash—read on for more on that). If the intent is more of a trailing off, you probably want an ellipsis.

Bridging Dashes
Bridging dashes connect two balloons or caption boxes. This is best used in spots where, if all the text were in a single block, there would be a midsentence dash—otherwise, a period or an ellipsis might be a better fit. If one element ends with a dash and the next one continues the same sentence, it's common to require a dash at the start of the next element.

Repeated Sounds
Most comics use a combination of double dashes (or em dashes) and single hyphens to indicate stammering, stuttering, and other types of repeated sounds. Specifically, publishers will commonly use a double dash or em dash if a whole word is being repeated ("You--you--"), including a single-letter word like "I," and a hyphen if it's a partial word ("Wh-what are y-you?"). Generally, the first letter after the dash or hyphen is capitalized only if it's the first letter of a proper noun ("N-New York").

En Dashes
The use of the en dash varies fairly widely. Some publishers and some comics do use it, though they might use it in a more limited list of contexts than *Chicago* would recommend (for example, in open compounds like "post–World War II" but not number ranges or vice versa). Others use hyphens for everything.

Note that British prose usually uses spaced en dashes for midsentence breaks ("It's better than bad – it's good!"). This can extend to UK comics—and comics following a UK-influenced style.

Hyphenated Compounds
In both AP and *Chicago* styles, most prefixes are closed up ("antimatter," "midyear," "subzero"). However, "super-" compounds describing special abilities, like "super-speed" and "super-hearing," are often hyphenated in comics even if words like "superhero," "superhuman," and "superpower" are closed. For other prefixes that might be singled out as exceptions to the default style manual or dictionary, see **Spelling**.

Hyphenation for other prefixes and compounds, including whether and when to hyphenate compound modifiers like "black-tie event" and "high school student," usually defers to the style manual.

Hyphens and Word Division
For the use of hyphens in breaking words across lines of text, see **Word Division** in chapter 4.

Other Dashes
Manga-inspired comics might use the Japanese wave dash, often represented in English-language publishing with the tilde (~), to indicate drawn-out speech or to punctuate sounds like sighs. (Non-English comics have all kinds of other punctuation conventions—see the manga-specific entries in the **Resources** lists for more.)

Ellipses
It's common in comics to use the ellipsis glyph (…), rather than individual periods as some types of publishing do. There are most often no spaces between the ellipsis and the surrounding text, which saves space in a space-limited medium.

IT'S…IT'S HERE!

    Some publishers use a space after an ellipsis if a speaker is trailing off and starting a new sentence. It's much rarer for a space to follow an ellipsis in all circumstances, and rarer still for spaces to appear on both sides.
    An ellipsis can also be used by itself in a balloon when someone is lost for words or communicating something through meaningful silence. With this usage, there may be more than three dots—some publishers have specific usage guidelines on how many, or it may vary from title to title or creator to creator. In vertical-scroll webtoons and comics translated from or influenced by languages (like Japanese) that use vertical writing, this type of ellipsis might be set vertically (⋮) rather than horizontally (…).

When an ellipsis is used at the beginning of a sentence and the lettering uses mixed case, the first word might or might not be capitalized. Any preferences should be noted in the style guide, but, as always, consistency one way or the other is king.

Bridging Ellipses
As with bridging dashes, if a balloon or caption box ends with a trailing ellipsis and the next one continues the sentence or thought, there's usually (but not always) an ellipsis at the start of that second balloon or box.

Exclamation Points
In most contexts, it's best to use a single exclamation point rather than multiple. This is true in prose publishing too, but comics lettering has even more options than plain text for emphasizing volume and intensity, like using bold italics or increasing the size of the text or balloon.

That said, multiple exclamation points do occasionally pop up. I usually recommend not using just two because it's likely to read as a typo—instead, you'll probably want either one or at least three.

One or more exclamation points might appear by themselves, either inside or outside a speech balloon, to communicate speechless surprise.

Periods

Because most comics use all-caps text, they usually use periods in some or all acronyms and initialisms for readability even if they otherwise follow *The Chicago Manual of Style* (which omits periods in most acronyms). Some publishers use periods only when it's necessary to distinguish an acronym from a regular word (like U.S. or S.H.I.E.L.D.) or individual initials from a name (like A.L.). Some use them in all-caps lettering but not mixed-case lettering. Others use them across the board for consistency.

Because of the space-constrained nature of comics, a publisher may also diverge from *Chicago*'s usual style for names with initials—while *Chicago* would use spaces after the periods in a name like J. R. R. Tolkien, a comics publisher may prefer J.R.R. Tolkien.

Punctuation and Dialogue

It's often a good idea to avoid certain punctuation marks in dialogue.

Parentheses are generally used to provide extra or explanatory information. When a character is interjecting an explanation into their own speech, this can often be better communicated through paired em dashes. If they're saying something as an aside, a letterer's use of text and balloon size, capitalization style, or fonts is often more effective.

Semicolons are a bit divisive. They sometimes feel overly formal in dialogue, and dashes or plain old periods are often a good alternative in those cases. It might also be appropriate to start a new speech balloon. On the other hand, they're a natural part of some writers' voices—especially in contexts like a scholarly character or a historical setting where being a little more formal makes sense. If semicolon use isn't covered by a comic's style sheet or a publisher's style guide, it's usually something to query first rather than change outright.

People sometimes pronounce punctuation when they talk. If a character is actually speaking a slash, it should be written out as, for example, "office-slash-lair." If a character is speaking scare quotes, it's commonly written as "quote-unquote." Comics will sometimes omit end punctuation, initial caps, or both with a short bit of dialogue (like a single word) or a sound appearing in a balloon by itself (like a laugh).

Question Marks

Like multiple exclamation points, it's best to avoid multiple question marks in a row. The text should generally use either a question mark followed by an exclamation point (see **Combined Punctuation**) or use size or emphasis to achieve the desired effect—or a combination of these.

Similar to exclamation points and ellipses, one or more question marks might appear by themselves to communicate speechless confusion.

Quotation Marks

As with apostrophes, quotation marks should be consistent in being styled as directional, a.k.a. curly or "smart" (usually preferred), or straight. Straight quotation marks are sometimes used to denote feet and inches, though the more proper symbols for this are the prime (′) and double prime (″) marks.

Quotation marks, like other punctuation in comic books, usually take the style of the text that precedes them. See **Emphasis** in the Formatting section for important information on how to apply this to paired punctuation like quotation marks when only one half of the pair is touching an emphasized element.

For the placement of commas, periods, and other punctuation relative to quotation marks, see **Combined Punctuation**.

Also see **Titles of Works** in the Formatting section.

Quotation Marks in Captions
One important place you might see quotation marks in comics is in captions representing dialogue from an off-panel speaker. This style is commonly used when a character in a story's present narrates a flashback over artwork of the past events or when a "preview" of the dialogue from the next scene is presented as a caption over the last panel of the current scene. (For more information on when and how captions are used, see **Captions, Notes, and Bursts**.)

> "I TRIED CALLING, BUT HE DIDN'T PICK UP...

> "...AND I WENT TO HIS HOUSE, BUT NO ONE WAS THERE.

> "HIS FAMILY HASN'T SEEN HIM IN WEEKS."

When speech in a caption is enclosed in quotation marks and continues across multiple caption boxes, the quotation marks follow a similar punctuation logic as multiple-paragraph quotes in prose books: There's an opening quotation mark at the start of each new paragraph (prose) or caption box (comics), but there's no closing quotation mark until the speaker finishes or is interrupted.

However, what counts as an interruption varies from publisher to publisher. Things that might or might not prompt a closing quotation mark include:

- dialogue by another character in the same place and time as the caption speaker
- dialogue *not* in the same place and time as the caption speaker (i.e., happening in the scene the character is speaking over)
- sound effects
- page breaks

There is also the situation where, for example, a character is narrating over a flashback and then we have a present-day panel that shows them finishing their story in a speech balloon. The last caption before that speech balloon might or might not get a closing quotation mark since it's the same speaker and the same continuous chunk of dialogue.

Quotation Marks in Balloons
When quotation marks appear within a speech balloon, they don't surround the whole text block the way dialogue is surrounded by quotation marks in a prose book—they're only used for quoted items within the speech, like song titles or sarcastic "scare quotes." Quotation marks in balloons are generally regular double quotation marks (unless you have nested quotes, in which case singles are used within doubles).

Combined Punctuation
An exclamation point with a question mark is probably the most common punctuation combo in comics. Unless the publisher has specified otherwise, the question mark comes first (?!). This is sometimes referred to as an interrobang, but technically that term refers to a combined single character (‽).

In North American publishing, it's standard for periods and commas to fall inside a closing quotation mark. An exclamation point, question mark, dash, or ellipsis might be inside or outside depending on whether it's part of the quoted text. A semicolon is always outside. You'll find more detailed rules in your style manual.

Some publishers allow ellipses and dashes to be combined with other punctuation, like periods and exclamation points, and others don't. Those that do allow it may have rules about whether the ellipsis or the other mark has to come first (…? and …! versus ?… and !…).

When an asterisk that indicates a footnote is adjacent to other punctuation, it should appear before an em dash or double dash. The asterisk should appear before a closing parenthesis if the note only applies to a specific part of the text inside the parentheses but after if it applies to everything inside the parentheses. It should follow any other punctuation.

See **Emphasis** for information on how combined punctuation next to bold italic text is handled.

COMMON PUNCTUATION ERRORS

Punctuation errors I see frequently include:

- backward apostrophes
- !? instead of ?! (when not allowed)
- incorrect quotation mark usage in dialogue captions
- missing direct address comma (when required by the style guide)
- improper use of double dash or hyphen for repeated sounds
- second ellipsis or dash missing in bridging punctuation (for style guides that require it)

NUMBERS

Numerals vs. Words 54
Subscript, Superscript, and Fractions 56
Numbers with Symbols 56
Number Ranges 57

Numerals vs. Words

It's very common for a comics publisher to have its own rules about when to spell out numbers and when to use numerals. Yes, some follow one of the standard *Chicago* or AP rule sets, like spelling out zero through nine and using numerals for everything else, but others spell out zero through twenty or treat numbers differently depending on whether they're hyphenated. It's also not uncommon to have different rules for numbers in lettered panels versus in cover copy, or captions versus dialogue.

In short, assume nothing. If you're a copyeditor or proofreader working with a publisher for the first time and the style guide doesn't specify, ask whether there's a preference.

Regardless of the overall number style, a publisher might choose to use numerals for all numbers in certain categories, regardless of size—such as measurements, ages, percentages, or scores. It might be worth considering additional exceptions on a case-by-case basis if a particular comic has a lot of numbers. Ordinal numbers also may be spelled out even when the corresponding cardinal number wouldn't be (for example, "30" but "thirtieth").

A number is often spelled out when it begins a sentence, but not always.

When multiple numbers of different sizes or categories appear near each other, you might end up with a situation where following the established rules would give you a mix of numerals and spelled-out numbers. It's good to be consistent within a balloon, panel, or page, but there isn't a single way to approach consistency. A publisher or creator might use numerals for all numbers in close proximity if the style would call for numerals for any of them ("She lives 20 miles outside town with her 6 cats"), or they might apply that only to numbers in the same category ("She lives 20 miles outside town with her six cats").

Other considerations for numbers include the following:

- Decimal amounts smaller than one usually include the zero before the decimal point for readability (0.1 rather than .1).
- Times of day might be spelled out or use numerals. If they use numerals, round times might use "o'clock," ":00," or neither with round times (2 o'clock, 2:00 p.m., 2 p.m.).
- Decades might use four digits (1980s), two digits ('80s), or words (eighties). When abbreviating decades, make sure the apostrophe is in the right place and facing the right way (see **Punctuation**).
- Roman numerals might or might not use crossbar I's (see **Capitalization**).

NUMBER PREFERENCES

Even if you follow your chosen style manual's default number rules to the letter, it's good practice to say so in your style guide because of how often this varies.

One category that might get overlooked in a style guide—but about which writers and readers who specialize in the genre tend to have strong preferences—is numbered military units. *Chicago* spells out everything through one hundred no matter the unit type, and AP uses Arabic numerals for all units, but when I worked for a (prose) military history imprint, we used Arabic numerals for things like battalions and divisions and Roman numerals for corps.

Subscript, Superscript, and Fractions

Comics often avoid subscript and superscript formatting, especially in all-caps lettering, because it can disrupt line heights and spacing or be too small to read comfortably. So it's not uncommon to see, for example, "H2O" rather than "H_2O." If it's used, superscript is usually not applied to ordinals (e.g., "20th," not "20th"), but some prefer it. Asterisks for editor's notes and other footnotes might or might not be superscript.

Subscript and superscript are sometimes used to create stacked fractions, especially if dedicated glyphs for the specific fractions don't exist as they do for more common amounts like ½. Leaving fractions as plain, unstacked text (e.g., 1/2) isn't ideal, but sometimes it's the best option. Here are examples of a "fake" stacked fraction created using superscript and subscript (A), the default glyph (B), and unstacked numbers (C) for the same fraction.

(A) $^1/_2$ CUP   (B) ½ CUP   (C) 1/2 CUP

Numbers with Symbols

Percentages might either use the % symbol or spell out "percent," or it might vary depending on whether the figure in question appears in dialogue or captions. Similarly, monetary amounts might be spelled out or might use numerals with the appropriate currency symbol. Temperatures and angles might use the degree symbol (°), but writing out "degrees" is common for readability.

When dimensions are set in numerals, they should use a multiplication symbol (e.g., 2×4), not the letter *x*, when possible. But not all comics fonts have this character (or the two may be indistinguishable), and some publishers and creators prefer the letter. Here's a comparison of how the same phrase looks with a multiplication sign (A), a small-cap letter (B), and a full-height letter (C).

(A) HIT HIM WITH A 2×4
(B) HIT HIM WITH A 2x4
(C) HIT HIM WITH A 2X4

Similarly, the prime (') and double prime (") marks are the proper symbols to denote feet and inches, but some people prefer straight single (') and double (") quotation marks.

Number Ranges

Numeral ranges might use a hyphen (1-10) or an en dash (1–10) depending on the style manual and style guide. For more on these marks, see **Dashes and Hyphens** in the Punctuation section.

Whichever character is used, it stands for "to," so "between 1–10" isn't correct—it should be "between 1 and 10" or just "1–10."

When a range is given for numerals with symbols, the symbol is typically used with both numbers ("issues #42–#47," "tickets are $20–$30"), but some publishers might choose to use it only with the first ("issues #42–47," "tickets are $20–30").

FORMATTING

Emphasis	57
Italics	59
Languages Other Than English	60
Personal Titles and Ranks	61
Possessives and Plurals	61
Script Styling	62
Sound Effects	62
Titles of Works	64
Other Text Effects	64

Emphasis

Comics tend to emphasize words in a way that would read as strange and over-the-top in something like a novel—in both frequency and formatting—but are normal, accepted style in this medium. Emphasis helps the reader quickly parse dialogue, communicates tone in the absence of cues like dialogue tags that you might see in other types of publishing, and, like many things, is a long-standing convention. The first appearance of a character's name in a comic is often emphasized (or styled as a logo), especially if it could be confused with a common noun.

For visibility, comics have historically used bold italic text for emphasis rather than just italics or just bold, though that's changed somewhat as printing quality has improved over the years and digital publishing has grown. (For other uses of plain italics, see **Italics**—next up in this section.) Plain bold is still fairly uncommon. Emphasized words may also be larger or a different color than the surrounding text, or all caps if the comic is lettered in mixed case.

Unlike in most prose books, the punctuation in comic books usually takes the style of the text that precedes it.

DON'T TELL ME. TELL **HER!**

When paired punctuation marks are involved, like quotation marks or parentheses, both marks in a pair will usually be set in the same style. There isn't a universal approach to which style is chosen when only one half of the pair is touching an emphasized element, but most often, the paired punctuation will only be emphasized if everything between them is emphasized (A); otherwise, they're both roman (B).

(A) THEY TOOK CARE OF A LITTLE **"PROBLEM"** IN TOWN.
(B) IF WE DON'T **MOVE**--AND MOVE FAST-- WE'RE DONE FOR.

There also isn't a universal rule for combined punctuation, but multiple punctuation marks in a row following an emphasized word are usually all emphasized (example C on the next page) unless one is half of a pair, in which case the previously described consistency rule will generally overrule this—in D, the exclamation point is bold, but the closing quotation mark is roman.

(C) TODAY IS **_TUESDAY?!_**
(D) SHE SAID, "YOU NEED TO GET HERE **_NOW!_**"

If you see a sentence where the emphasis seems like it's on the wrong word or syllable based on the way it would be spoken, this is usually worth flagging whether you're copy-editing or proofreading.

Italics

Even in a comic that uses bold italics rather than just italics for emphasis, plain italics still have their place.

Sometimes, whole caption boxes or speech balloons of a certain type will be italicized as a global style. You might see this for narration, singing, whispering, or radio balloons. (See the **Balloons** section in chapter 4 for an explanation of radio balloons and other special types.) A comic may also use italics for words in breath marks or small utterances like "Hmm" and "Huh."

When house style is to italicize things like book titles, ship names, and Latin species names, these generally get regular italics, not bold italics. On the other hand, standard *Chicago* style is to italicize "letters as letters" and "words as words," but you're more likely to see bold italic or quotation marks in comics.

Punctuation surrounding italicized text might also be italicized, following the same approach as punctuation surrounding emphasized text, or it might only be italicized if it's part of a title or other italic element.

For italics with non-English words and phrases, see **Styling Non-English Text** under the next entry.

Languages Other Than English

Angle brackets are a common convention that indicates speech is supposed to be happening in a language other than the overall language of the story—like something between subtitles and everyone in a movie speaking English even though it's taking place in revolutionary France. Generally, this is introduced with a footnote on their first appearance that indicates, for example, "Translated from French." As with breath marks, the text within angle brackets is sometimes italicized.

Brackets aren't the only option, of course. A writer or letterer might use another punctuation mark (like guillemets « ») or a special style (like a different color or font) to signal non-English text.

If there's only a non-English word or sentence here and there in a comic, you may not need any of these approaches—using the non-English text in the balloon and providing a translation in a footnote or elsewhere (or even no translation at all) can work fine for limited applications. But once you have a significant amount of text in another language, this gets unwieldy very quickly unless you're writing for a presumed bilingual reader or portraying a situation where a character or the reader isn't supposed to understand everything (Matt Fraction and David Aja's *Hawkeye* #19 being a prominent example).

If there's a fictional language represented by a fictional writing system, the writer or letterer should provide their editor, copyeditor, or proofreader with a key, if one exists, so they can spot potential errors and inconsistencies.

Styling Non-English Text
When a book includes actual non-English text rather than using a translation mechanic, some languages will require decisions about style and spelling. For example, a long vowel in Japanese could use either a macron (ō) or a circumflex (ô), among other differences, depending on what romanization system you're using. Whether this comes up often enough to be documented in a publisher's style guide or is something handled on a case-by-case basis will depend on the content they publish.

Although a lot of style manuals used to recommend italicizing non-English words and phrases appearing in English-language text, there's been a movement away from this for quite a while because it can be seen as unnecessarily singling out the words. Unless something is likely to be confused with an English word of the same spelling or you're intentionally emphasizing the foreignness of a word—like someone ostentatiously pronouncing the name of a dish at an Italian restaurant to sound fancy—I recommend treating everything the same.

Personal Titles and Ranks
Ranks and titles like "Dr.," "Mr.," and "Lt." might be abbreviated before a name in general usage but are often spelled out when they're part of superhero names, like Doctor Strange or Mister Miracle. They will also typically be spelled out when appearing alone ("Yes, Doctor").

For capitalization of titles, see the **Capitalization** section.

Possessives and Plurals
Whether you write "Jones' house" and "Martinez' car" or "Jones's house" and "Martinez's car" will depend on your style guide and style manual.

Apostrophes usually aren't used to form plurals, but in all-caps lettering, plurals of individual letters might use apostrophes ("P'S AND Q'S"), small caps ("Ps AND Qs"), or both. In mixed case, lowercase plural letters usually need apostrophes for readability ("p's and q's"); capital plurals often don't ("Ps and Qs") but sometimes do ("crossbar I's," to distinguish from the word "Is"). Also see **Italics** for "letters as letters."

As mentioned under **Capitalization**, a small-cap or lowercase s is also sometimes used to pluralize acronyms, initialisms, and numbers in all-caps lettering.

Script Styling

Different publishers (and letterers) have different preferences on how a script is formatted, but there are usually a few commonalities.

As mentioned under **Capitalization**, the dialogue, captions, and other text to be lettered should be set in mixed case even if the comic will be lettered in all caps. Among other things, this sets the text up correctly for crossbar I's, creating much less work for the letterer. For similar reasons, the publisher might request that the writer use plain bold or bold underline rather than bold italics for emphasized text, even if it will be lettered in bold italic, in order to better set it apart from text that is only italicized.

See **chapter 3** for a full overview of script formatting and editing.

Sound Effects

Sound effects (SFX) refer to sounds that aren't part of the dialogue, like the boom of an explosion or the ring of a doorbell. They're generally set in standalone lettering rather than in any kind of balloon or box, and they might be created by the letterer, the artist(s), or a combination of both. They most often take the form of onomatopoeias—whether dictionary words like *crash* and *hiss*, phonetic spellings like *krakow* and *fwump*, or a mix.

These elements might or might not be the copyeditor's or proofreader's responsibility to check. In most cases, writers, letterers, and artists have practically infinite leeway when it comes to sound effects—they don't need to follow standard spelling or punctuation or even stick with the same conventions within a single comic. But that doesn't mean the editor or proofreader can't still watch for spelling oddities (like a letter that doesn't seem to fit in context), a sound effect that doesn't match the sound it's indicating (like a glass making a clinking noise when it hits the floor even though it's carpeted), or a combination of letters that inadvertently spells out a word the creator didn't intend (especially a naughty one).

It's worth keeping in mind that changing even a single letter in a sound effect is usually much more labor intensive if it's part of the art than if the letterer created it. It won't always be obvious to a proofreader which person created which elements, but if an effect is clearly part of the artwork, it's a good idea to ask yourself whether a change is really, truly necessary before marking it.

Silent "Sound Effects"

Sometimes, sound effect styling will be used for words that aren't meant to indicate audible sounds but instead things like moods, states of being, or silent actions—like "anger," "cold," or "stare." These are often inspired by manga, where they're known as *gitaigo* (for physical states or motions) and *gijōgo* (for feelings or mental states).

Titles of Works

Different style manuals have different rules about when to use italics, quotation marks, or neither for the names of different types of works. But while those will cover titles of series, stories, movies, and other things that might come up, they won't include guidance for comics "events" or arcs.

The definitions of these terms are somewhat fluid, but an event usually refers to a major storyline taking place across multiple series from a publisher—like "The Death of Superman," which involved *Superman*, *Action Comics*, and other series. An arc usually refers to a storyline taking place across multiple issues of a single series, like "Born Again" in *Daredevil*, or sometimes a story phase within an event.

Because both events and arcs are, in a sense, part of an overall series, there's an argument to be made for treating them like short story or episode titles, which usually take quotation marks—a story that only spans a single issue, or part of one, is usually treated that way. But you could also argue that something uniting multiple issues, or even multiple separate series, is on a large enough scale that it makes more sense to treat it like a book or series title, which means italicizing it if you're following *Chicago* style rules. (And, of course, an event or arc might be published as a collected edition under the same name.) Or a publisher or creator might decide that since these elements don't fall neatly into one category, using title capitalization but no special formatting is the way to go for one or both.

For capitalization of titles, see **Title Case**.

Other Text Effects

Letterers have a variety of other options at their disposal to give the text a particular feel. They may play with type size, baseline shift, the angle of a line or individual letters, or using "hollow" letters. For more on lettering, see **chapter 4**.

COMMON FORMATTING ERRORS

Some of the most common formatting errors I see are:

- punctuation surrounding bold italic text not being bold italic
- incorrect possessive form for a name ending in s or z
- inconsistent use of italics for text in breath marks or other small utterances
- missing formatting (e.g., italics or quotation marks, depending on the style guide or style manual) for the title of a book or movie

CAPTIONS, NOTES, AND BURSTS

Voiceover 66
Time and Place Captions 67
Notes 68
Signs, Letters, and Screens 68
Special Shapes 68

Caption can mean very different things depending on what type of publishing you're talking about. In comics, it refers to lettered text that appears in a box or is otherwise set off from the artwork and balloons.

    Captions serve a lot of different functions. They can be used for narration. They can be used to tell the reader when and where a scene is taking place. They can be used in place of thought balloons or when the character speaking isn't part of the scene the art is depicting. And then there's text from letters and screens, explanatory notes, and more.

    Some comics will use one style of caption box for all of these, but many will use different styles for different applications. For example, there might be one style for narration and a different style for spoken dialogue—whether that means a different box shape, decoration, color scheme, text alignment, typeface, or all of the above. Even within a single category, a comic might use different colors or icons for different characters so it's obvious who's talking even if there's no other context to indicate this.

In American-style comic books and graphic novels, captions are more often than not—but not always—enclosed in boxes. Webcomics may be more likely than "traditional" print comics to use unbounded caption text (or dialogue, for that matter).

Voiceover

Voiceover can refer to a few different things in comics. Some people apply the term to everything I'll discuss here, but some people just apply it to narration.

Off-Panel Dialogue

When a character is speaking from out of frame, there are a variety of ways to indicate this depending on the position of the character relative to the scene and the preferences of the letterer or editor. One is a balloon with a tail coming from out of frame, indicating the person is just out of view but audible to whoever's shown in the panel. Another is a balloon with no tail, which can have a few different uses depending on the creator or publisher (see **Styles and Uses** in the Balloons section in chapter 4).

But if the character who's speaking isn't actually part of the scene the artwork is showing, the dialogue will often be enclosed in quotation marks and set in a caption box. This comes up most commonly in two situations: one, when a person is narrating a flashback; and two, when the reader starts "hearing" dialogue from the next scene over the last panel of the current scene or, conversely, the last dialogue of the outgoing scene overlies the first panel of the next scene (what would be called a *J cut* and *L cut* or *prelap* and *postlap* in screenwriting). For the proper use of quotation marks with dialogue that continues across multiple captions, see **Quotation Marks** in the Punctuation section.

Narration
Nondiegetic narration—narration that only the reader "hears" and that isn't happening in the world of the story—serves a similar function to something like a character narrating a flashback, but it's a frame for the whole book rather than an individual scene. It usually doesn't use quotation marks, but it might be italicized or have other special styling.

Thoughts
Some comics still use the classic "bubble" thought balloon, but creators have increasingly moved away from that style in favor of putting characters' thoughts in caption boxes. These tend to be styled more like narration than off-panel dialogue in that they usually don't use quotation marks and are often italicized.

Time and Place Captions
Another important use for captions is establishing location or time of a scene. These can be absolute ...

LONDON, 8:00 A.M.

... or relative.

MEANWHILE...
ELSEWHERE...

A caption might give both the place and time or just one or the other. They don't use quotation marks and usually end with either a period or an ellipsis. Location captions are sometimes referred to as *locators*.

Although these types of captions might appear in the same kind of boxes as the others, they're often not enclosed in boxes at all, instead using a different kind of display type style to set them off.

Mixed-case time/place captions might be capitalized either title style or sentence style. Less commonly, a design decision might be made to use all lowercase or some other style.

Notes
Another use for caption boxes is for footnotes, such as an editor's note explaining that an event the characters are talking about happened in another issue or episode (see the example on page 45) or that dialogue is being "translated" from another language (example on page 60). Although a note might appear at the bottom of the page in paginated comics, it's very common for it to appear instead at the bottom of the panel in which the asterisk appears.

Signs, Letters, and Screens
While things like signage, handwritten letters, and emails might be part of the art, the text can also be pulled out and displayed as a caption for easier reading or to let the artwork focus on other elements. These will usually have their own style distinct from other types of captions.

Dearest Zebulon,
By the time you read this...

how did you get this number?

Special Shapes
Text can also appear in bursts and a variety of other containers. Among other things, these might be used for sound effects (think of the classic "Pow!"), for extra information about characters or objects, or for fourth-wall-breaking commentary. There isn't a universal approach for how to style the text inside these elements, but they should generally be consistent among a given type.

SPECIAL SYMBOLS

Breath Marks 69
Grawlixes and Censor Bars 70
Logos 71
Music 71

Note: For mathematical symbols, see the **Numbers** section.

Breath Marks

Breath marks, often called *whiskers*,* frame sounds like sighs, grunts, coughs, and other vocalizations that aren't speech. They may follow different style conventions from the rest of the dialogue in a comic, such as using italics or mixed case. They may or may not use end punctuation. There may be house rules about whether both real words (*cough*) and phonetic onomatopoeias (*koff*) are acceptable, and whether the sounds have to be "breath" sounds. As with most things, consistency is most important.

≈ WHEEZE! ≈

    Some comics use asterisks instead of breath marks (*sigh*), usually without spaces. This tends to be more common in webcomics and those influenced by manga, manhua, and manhwa.
    Breath marks and asterisks might appear on their own or between sentences, or they might interrupt speech. They might even appear without any text between them at all. Brackets of one type or another might indicate breath marks in a script (>gasp< {huff} [wheeze]), but if these characters appear in a lettered comic, they should be flagged—it's probably an error.

---

* Also crow's feet, roach legs, or fireflies.

Grawlixes and Censor Bars

Comics for teens and younger audiences usually limit how much profanity they include, so it's common to use grawlixes (the classic mash of symbols—sometimes also called profanitype or obscenicons) or censor bars to block out curse words.

WHAT THE %#&@ ARE YOU DOING HERE?

WHAT THE ▓▓▓▓ ARE YOU DOING HERE?

Specific combinations of characters might or might not consistently map onto the same profanities. Depending on the publisher's or writer's preference, a copyeditor or proofreader might just need to keep an eye out for anything that doesn't sufficiently censor the word (say, @$$ for "ass"), or they might be asked to make sure the text follows specific conventions or patterns of symbols.

Solid bars might be a design element applied individually to each censored word rather than a character style applied directly to the type, so the proofreader should always check each one and not assume that if one is perfect, they all will be.

There are infinite other ways a letterer might censor text as well—for example, dialogue looking like it's scribbled out in the speech balloon. Similar to the way ellipses can be used by themselves, you might see a speech balloon with nothing but a scribble in it to indicate angry silence or unintelligible grumbling instead of a censored word.

Even in a mature-rated book that uses uncensored profanity, it's worth thinking carefully about whether to write out things like slurs in full. Obviously, you sometimes have a terrible character saying terrible things, but writing the word out may do more to hurt readers who belong to the group it's used against than to demonstrate how bad the character is. Important factors to consider include whether the writer belongs to that community and how the slur is treated within the story. (For example, does it pass by unaddressed? Or is it explicitly framed as objectionable, such as through another character immediately calling it out?)

Although it's the writer and the editor—and sometimes others up the publishing chain of command—who make this decision, I encourage copyeditors and proofreaders to speak up if they see something that could affect the audience in ways the creative team might not have intended.

For more on spelling out swear words, see **Profanity** in the Spelling section.

Logos

Sometimes, when a character (especially a superhero) is introduced or mentioned for the first time in a comic, their name will appear as a wordmark logo within the text. If this convention is being used, it's important to ensure the comic is consistent in terms of both when logos appear for what characters and what a specific character's logo looks like.

Music

If someone is singing or listening to music,* the words are usually set off with musical notes, a different text style (often italics), or both. Like sound effects, these might be created by either the letterer or the artists. You could also see a balloon with only musical notes and no words in it, which might indicate whistling or humming.

---

* Using copyrighted lyrics in fiction is its own topic and a matter for intellectual property lawyers. Suffice it to say that if a song isn't in the public domain, permission is nearly always required—often from multiple people—and it can be prohibitively expensive.

SPELLING

Accents and Dialects 72
Brands 73
Creator Names 73
Profanity 75
Slang and Online Conventions 76

Accents and Dialects

Because speech in comics stands by itself, without any help from dialogue tags and other descriptions that something like a novel might have, it can be tempting to communicate a character's accent or other characteristics through spelling. But there's a fine line between phonetic spelling that effectively communicates an accent and text that's a chore to read.

In addition, all people have some kind of accent, and choosing to represent one with special spelling and not another carries weight and may imply judgment—or worse, especially if an accent is inaccurate or unintentionally exaggerated. As former Random House copy chief Benjamin Dreyer puts it in *Dreyer's English*, "At best you'll come off as classist and condescending; at worst, in some cases, you'll tip over into racism. A lot can be accomplished with word choice and word order. Make good use of those." Books like *The Chicago Guide to Copyediting Fiction* and *Self-Editing for Fiction Writers* and some helpful online articles include guidance on walking this line—see **Resources**.

One caveat: When a writer is representing their own dialect—whether through spelling, word choice, or grammar—it's important for a copyeditor or proofreader who isn't a speaker of that dialect to be aware that it might follow different rules from "standard" English.

Brands

The biggest publishers have dedicated reviewers or even whole departments that will check content for possible issues that could arise from featuring real-life brands in a story. This book isn't the place to get into the boundaries of fair use, but it should ideally be made clear at the outset of a project whether a copyeditor is expected to flag any real brands for further review. By the time a book gets to the proofreader, all of this should theoretically be sorted out (though it never hurts to ask if you see something questionable), but the proofreader may instead be asked to watch for brands that are part of the artwork.

A publisher might have preferences different from the default in its chosen style manual about how brands, including the names of other publishers, are styled. For example, is a company's choice to style its name in all caps followed, or does everything get initial caps only? (Also, see **Proper Nouns and "The"** in the Capitalization section.)

Copyright and trademark symbols generally aren't required (or desirable) unless the brand in question is the publisher or licensor of the content, which, like fair use, is a whole different topic. Licensors will reliably have their own style and branding guides that lay out acceptable use—not just spelling and trademark symbols but whether a brand name can be used as a noun or a product can be portrayed in certain contexts in text or artwork. A licensor will typically have a person or team responsible for reviewing content to ensure it follows these guidelines, but a copyeditor or proofreader may also be given this information to check as part of their work.

Creator Names

Obviously, it's critically important for the names of all writers, artists, letterers, and others to be spelled correctly in the comics they create. A copyeditor should verify all proper nouns as part of their work, but sometimes there's conflicting information online, or there are two creators with similar names.

Beyond that, there are house standards to consider. Does the publisher apply a standard style when it comes to periods and spacing in names with initials, or do creator preferences prevail? Are things like initials or accents treated differently in all caps than they are in mixed case? When names with internal capitalization appear in all caps, do they get small caps for better readability? Do the names of creators from countries where the family name comes first appear in that order or Western order? Ideally, decisions like these should be documented in the house style guide or as part of a master list of creator names.

When it comes to proofreading, it's important to be clear on scope and responsibilities. Generally speaking, it's a proofreader's job to check correct spelling against provided reference materials but not to look up personal names or other proper nouns in outside sources; the copyeditor or publisher should have compiled the relevant information on the style sheet or in a global list like the one described under "Building a Creator Name Database," below. That said, sometimes a publisher will specifically request outside checking. I encourage any proofreader who doesn't receive information on creator names as part of a project's documents to check with their contact and make sure everyone's on the same page.

Building a Creator Name Database
Some publishers maintain official lists of the proper spellings for the creators they work with. This is an incredibly helpful practice that not only saves copyeditors and proofreaders time but ensures they know the correct form for any name they might come across. Either the list can be provided to editorial freelancers in its entirety or just the relevant creator names can be provided for an individual project's style sheet. There are lots of important details to be mindful of in addition to the literal order of the letters.

- If a person has a last name beginning with an article like "de" or "von," is the article capitalized or lowercase? (And is there a space between the article and the rest of the name?)
- Does the creator use their middle initial(s) in credits?
- If the creator uses a full given name in some contexts and a nickname or initials in others, which form is preferred when?
- Are there diacritical (accent) marks? And if so, which way do they face—for example, é or è?
- Are there intercaps? (e.g., MacGregor)
- If a name has multiple parts, are they separated by a hyphen, a space, or neither? (Mary Anne vs. MaryAnne, Stevens Johnson vs. Stevens-Johnson)
- Does the creator use all caps or all lowercase?
- If the creator has an alias or brand name, are both used in credits, or just one? If both, how is this styled? (Setting the nickname in quotation marks is a commonly used option, whether between the given and family names or following the whole name in parentheses.)
- Has the creator's name changed since you first started working with them? If so, should their previous name remain as is on reprints of older work, or should it be updated?
- When a creator team sharing a last name is credited, should they be "Jack and Mary Smith" or "Jack Smith and Mary Smith"?

Profanity

Although some comics censor swear words (see **Grawlixes and Censor Bars** under Special Symbols), others use them freely. This leads to the question of how to style certain profanities, especially compounds: Is it "shit-faced" or "shitfaced"? "Damn it" or "damnit" or "dammit"? Merriam-Webster and other dictionary publishers cover some profanities, but the more creative the swear, the less likely it is to be documented.

Green's Dictionary of Slang is a great resource for both historical and modern profanity, including slurs. The BuzzFeed Style Guide is also helpful for more recent slang, especially if you're debating how to spell or punctuate something. (A caveat: It's not clear how long it will stay online given that it was created by the BuzzFeed News copy desk, and the whole news arm of the website was shuttered in 2023.) And there's the helpful booklet *A Very Sweary Dictionary*, published by UK-based editor Kia Thomas in 2020—especially helpful if you're working with a British character, but a lot of the terms are applicable to both sides of the pond—and the blog *Strong Language*.

Different sources will inevitably disagree in places, but when in doubt, one thing to keep in mind is that compounds usually trend toward closed forms over time—"cock-block" tends to become "cockblock," just as "good-bye" has mostly become "goodbye." So if you're on the fence about something, I almost always recommend closing it up unless it could create an issue with readability.

Also note the recommendation on slurs under **Grawlixes and Censor Bars** in the Special Symbols section.

Slang and Online Conventions

As with profanity, Green's Dictionary of Slang and the BuzzFeed Style Guide are good resources. On the other hand, Urban Dictionary isn't especially useful, since anyone can add entries—and some entries are only there as jokes. Gretchen McCulloch's book *Because Internet* can be helpful with online-specific slang and conventions for grammar, spelling, and punctuation.

HOUSE SPELLING

In addition to specifying which style manual your copyeditors and proofreaders should follow, you'll want to choose a dictionary. While some things are spelling errors no matter who you ask, lots of other words have multiple acceptable forms but might not be covered by the *Chicago Manual* or AP. Merriam-Webster is a common and widely respected choice among editors, but it's hardly the only option. And be sure to specify a version—the free online dictionary at merriam-webster.com has some differences from *Merriam-Webster's Collegiate*.

And the decision-making doesn't stop there. Dictionaries will list multiple acceptable options for some words and phrases. Do you always want to use the first one listed, or is either one fine as long as it's consistent within a given comic or series?

Beyond that, a publisher might just want to spell, punctuate, or capitalize certain words differently than the default dictionary or style manual would. Plus, not every word will be listed in your chosen dictionary at all.

All of these preferences should be documented in your style guide. Here are some words for which preference questions often come up.

- AKA *or* a.k.a. (for mixed case)
- all right *or* alright
- arch-enemy *or* archenemy
- backup *or* back-up (noun or adjective)
- bestseller, bestselling *or* best seller, best-selling
- catalog, dialog, etc. *or* catalogue, dialogue
- cause, 'cause, cuz, *or* cos (for "because")
- code name *or* codename (and, if writing it as two words, should the verb be code-name?)
- comic *or* comics (as an adjective—do you say "comic artist" or "comics artist"?)
- comms *or* coms

(continued on next page)

- course *or* 'course (for "of course")
- crime fighter, crime-fighter, *or* crimefighter
- damn it, dammit, *or* damnit
- dox, doxed *or* doxx, doxxed
- earth, Earth (you might use the first for the general sense of "soil" and the other for the planet, or you might use the same style for both)
- face to face *or* face-to-face (adverb)
- geez *or* jeez
- home world *or* homeworld
- IDed, ID'd, *or* ID'ed
- high jinks *or* hijinks
- klick *or* click (for kilometer)
- oh my god, oh my God, *or* omigod
- OK/O.K. *or* okay
- on board *or* onboard (adverb)
- penciler, penciling *or* penciller, pencilling
- ret-con *or* retcon
- sci fi *or* sci-fi (noun)
- shape-shift *or* shapeshift
- space-time *or* spacetime
- till *or* 'til (*Chicago* prefers "till," which is actually an older word than "until"—just don't use both an apostrophe *and* two l's)
- time travel *or* time-travel (verb)
- under way *or* underway (adverb)
- whadaya, whaddya, *or* whadja, etc. (also whatcha)
- world-building, worldbuilding
- y'know, ya know, *or* yanno
- zero-G, zero G, *or* zero g

Here are some prefixes that might not be covered by your style manual or that you might want to handle differently than the style manual suggests:

- co- (co-creator *or* cocreator?)
- meta- (meta-human *or* metahuman?)
- off- (off-world *or* offworld?)
- super- (super-speed *or* superspeed? super-powered *or* superpowered?)

3
COPYEDITING SCRIPTS

IN THIS CHAPTER:

The Case for Copyediting	81
Copyediting Scope	82
Script Format	84
Editing Tips	90

Before they're illustrated and lettered panels, many comics start as scripts that lay out what the artwork should look like and what text should be lettered.

Creators who do everything themselves might skip the script stage, especially if they're self-publishing or their comic is short. And even if different people are handling the words, artwork, and lettering, there are teams that prefer a similar "art first" approach, which might mean text is instead drafted over roughs (preliminary sketches laying out the panels and art), pencils, or inks before it goes to an editor.

As I've mentioned throughout this book, comics often don't go through a dedicated copyediting pass even when there is a script. The editor working with the writer on the story and art direction might copyedit the text as part of their work, or there might not be any copyediting at all. (More on this in a minute.)

This chapter is for those cases where a script does get some form of copyediting. I'll go through some of the dos, don'ts, and key components that someone copyediting a script should be aware of—whether they're a freelancer doing only that or an in-house editor doing it as part of their other work.

An in-house editor or assistant might be reporting to another editor or working directly with the author. A freelance copyeditor might be working with an editor, writer, do-it-all creator, publisher, freelance manager, or someone else entirely. To keep things simple, I've used *client* throughout this chapter to talk about whoever will be reviewing copyedits and making decisions on the script.

THE CASE FOR COPYEDITING

It tends to be unpopular to suggest a dedicated copyediting pass for comics. In many cases, I agree it's unnecessary—if the word count is low or the main editor on a comic is themselves a solid copyeditor or proofreader, it might not make sense. There's also the simple fact that for something like an ongoing series with a tight schedule, or a comic whose writing will be significantly revised for page or panel fit after it's been lettered, it might not be possible regardless of whether anyone on the team would want it.

On the other hand, if the main editor isn't a style guide expert or a comic is long or complex, copyediting can save time, money, and headaches and help make it the best it can be.

Efficiency

A good copyeditor can catch style, spelling, grammar, and consistency errors at the point in the process when they're easiest to fix, making less work for the proofreader and letterer and ensuring they can focus on other things. The more time a letterer has to spend on making editorial corrections, the less time they have to make sure that, for example, all the balloons and sound effects are perfect—and if there are too many corrections, the publisher might have to pay the letterer extra or make the changes in-house.

Errors

The more changes you make at the lettering stage, the more chances there are for a mistake to be missed—a proofreader is much more likely to catch all the errors if there are five of them than if there are fifty—or accidentally introduced in the process.

Besides the mechanics, copyeditors can also catch issues with continuity, clarity, anachronisms, and other aspects that might be even more difficult and expensive to fix once the comic has already been inked, colored, and lettered.

Respect

Aside from all these ways copyediting can benefit the publisher, sending the letterer a script that's as clean as possible is the respectful thing to do. Letterers are typically paid a page rate (or a comparable fee structure for webcomics) based on their experience and how much time the project is expected to take; if there are more corrections than expected, it will add time without adding any compensation.

A proofreader might be paid by page, by flat fee, or by hour. But even if they're paid more for the extra time they spend on corrections, they've probably reserved a certain amount of time in their schedule based on the expected amount of work.

See **chapter 1** for more information on how the copyeditor fits into the publishing workflow and how copyeditors and clients can collaborate for the best work. See the **Does It Need a Copyedit?** sidebar at the end of this chapter for what factors to consider if you're thinking about skipping a copyedit.

COPYEDITING SCOPE

Because copyediting isn't a universal part of the comics publishing process, there isn't a universal definition of what it includes, so it's important to establish the specifics of the work at the outset of a project.

What Parts Get Copyedited?

The most fundamental question to answer is which text should and shouldn't be edited. Most often, the copyeditor will only be editing the text that's going to be lettered—the dialogue, captions, sound effects, and so on—and not the stage directions or descriptive elements. But a client might choose to copyedit the whole script, sometimes in anticipation of it being published on its own at some point or adapted into an audio version.

Besides the question of whether these elements should be edited for spelling and grammar, there's also the question of formatting them on the page. A client might ask the copyeditor to format the document as part of their work—i.e., not just things like bold and italics in the text to be lettered, but how the panel descriptions and so on are indented or sized. If so, they should provide guidance as to what format to follow. On the other hand, if you've confirmed that this isn't part of your work, you should consider these elements outside your domain; a copyeditor might think tidying up the grammar and consistency of the scene descriptions is helpful, but to the client it could be unnecessary visual clutter or, worse, a major professional overstep.

Defining Copyediting

As in any medium, copyediting is a spectrum. Light copyediting focuses on straightforward errors, whereas heavier copyediting might also include suggestions for word choice or phrasing. It can also include things like continuity and fact-checking.

Plot and character development are generally the purview of the editor, but a copyeditor should keep an eye out for any consistency and continuity issues—for example, a character describing an event as having happened that morning when the captions say three days have passed—unless told otherwise.

If a comic is meant for young readers, the copyeditor might be asked to flag language that's inappropriate for the target reading level.

The copyeditor might also be asked to flag brand names or enforce particular style rules related to a licensor—see the **Brands** part of the Spelling section in chapter 2 for more.

A copyeditor should create a style sheet for any project they edit. See **chapter 2** for more information about style sheets and the **appendix** for an example.

Overediting

Comics are often heavy on dialogue and casual in style, and copyeditors should always keep voice and tone in mind. It might make sense to correct a character's grammar if they're a university English professor but less so if they're a five-year-old kid. You might query a scientific inconsistency in a hard sci-fi epic but not in a comedy story that clearly doesn't care about following the laws of physics.

And although this book lays out common conventions and recommends some best practices, these aren't the only ways to do things. If a script consistently goes against something in this or another chapter, query it before making a global change—the client might want it the way it is.

SCRIPT FORMAT

Unlike screenplays, which widely follow a single accepted format, comics scripts vary in style from writer to writer and publisher to publisher. That said, there are some common elements you can expect, and I'll lay them out in the rest of this chapter.

Some scripts are more casual and conversational; others are rigidly formal. Some include extensive descriptions for the artists and letterers; others are very bare-bones. The writer might embed reference or inspiration images right in the document. How any individual script looks will be driven by the relationship between the writer and the artist(s), the requirements of the publisher, and how much sway a writer has to dictate their own preferences, among other factors.

I've included one sample excerpt later in this chapter, but writer Kenny Porter has a helpful guide to some of the other common styles in use on his blog. Letterers Nate Piekos and Todd Klein also have some best practices and styling tips on their websites. Chapter 3 of Shelly Bond's *Filth and Grammar* discusses scripts from the editor's perspective.

Additionally, browsing real scripts uploaded to the Comic Book Script Archive or Comics Experience Script Archive will give you an idea of how formats can vary in practice and allow you to get familiar with what you might be working with. Some published collected editions that incorporate behind-the-scenes material also include partial or complete scripts. A copyeditor is generally expected to roll with what they're given, but clarity is always important—if it's not clear to you whether something is meant to be lettered text or instructions for the letterer or artist, ask.

File Type

Copyediting in Microsoft Word using Track Changes is standard, though some creators and publishers prefer Google Docs, rich text format (RTF), or other word processing options.

A letterer will apply bold and italic fonts to text manually, so scripts usually use Word's default font options for this formatting, but there are exceptions. If a comic has a significant amount of text that incorporates bolding or italics and will be typeset rather than lettered—say, a series of introductory essays—the person doing that typesetting might prefer that it use Word Styles or ScML markup, since that coding can be automatically mapped onto specific styles in InDesign. (For more on the differences between typesetting and lettering, see **chapter 4**.)

Vocabulary

There should ideally be a key at the beginning of the script laying out abbreviations the writer is using and what they mean, or a publisher might have a standard set all writers are meant to use. This helps ensure that the editor, copyeditor, and letterer all understand what's intended.

Here are some common examples:

- BG: background
- cap: caption
- CU: close-up
- ext: exterior
- FG: foreground
- int: interior
- off or OP: off-panel (you might also see the screenwriting abbreviations OC and OS, for "off-camera" and "off-screen")
- pn: panel
- POV: point of view

- SFX (or just FX): sound effect
- sm: small text
- sotto or SV: sotto voce (i.e., quietly or under the breath)
- VO: voiceover
- whspr: whispering

Comics scripts can use a lot of the same terminology as screenplays, and some use the same format as well. Reading up on screenwriting vocab will help you understand unfamiliar "stage directions" or descriptions.

It's also good to know some of the common terms used to describe panels and pages:

- bleed: artwork placement in which the image extends all the way to the edge of the page or screen (or the part of that artwork that could be trimmed off in the printing process)
- gutter: the space outside the panels (or, in print publishing, the part of any page closest to the binding)
- inset: a panel within a panel
- splash: a large "hero" panel that takes up anywhere from most of a page to a full spread in print, a full screen or more in a webtoon, or a comparably large space in another webcomic format
- spread: two facing pages
- tier: a horizontal row of panels

The Creator's Guide to Comics Devices is a great resource for more terms related to layout.

Capitalization and Crossbars

Scripts often use all caps for elements like dialogue assignments and page or panel headings. But even if a comic will be lettered in all caps, the dialogue, captions, and any other text that will be lettered should usually be set in mixed case. In most all-caps lettering fonts, typing a lowercase *i* creates a slash I and typing a capital *I* creates a crossbar I, so if a letterer pasted an all-caps script into their design program, every *I* in the whole comic would have crossbars. That would mean they'd have to manually change all the ones that shouldn't have them—which is most of them—to slashes.

Because of this, you might see a lowercase *i* in a comics script in a place that looks wrong, like the beginning of a sentence or the middle of an otherwise all-caps word or acronym. Unless it's a personal pronoun or another placement where the client has indicated they use a crossbar I, like Roman numerals, it's probably intentional. Not all publishers and creators do this, but it can be a huge help to the letterer.

Of course, if a comic will be lettered in mixed case or will use slash I's throughout, this treatment might not be needed, and the script can be capitalized normally. And, as mentioned under **Copyediting Scope**, if a copyeditor receives a script that's set consistently in all caps, they should make sure they know what the client wants before charging ahead and making everything mixed case.

Script Anatomy

Here is a simplified example of what you might see on the script page.

PAGE 12 **A** (4 PANELS)

Panel 1—outside the spaceship **B**
RICO and JAX look around suspiciously.

1. **C** CAP (TIME/PLACE)
Meanwhile...

2. RICO **D**
E is someone there?

Panel 2
RICO and JAX jump at a loud noise from off-panel.

3. SFX **F**
Kra-kow! **G**

4. JAX (whisper) **H**
<What was that?>*

5. CAPTION
*Translated from Neptunian.

6. **I** JAX (whisper)
It sounded like a blaster!

Panel 3
Close on RICO and JAX.

7. RICO (whisper)
>pfft< **J** Like I can see any better than you!

Panel 4
Maris's voice suddenly blares over the communicator hanging on JAX's belt.

8. SFX
crackle

9. MARIS (electric)
Everything okay out there?

A Pagination, when present, refers to the pages in the finished comic and not necessarily the page number in the script document. (It may take more than a document page to describe one comics page.) The page heading is often larger, underlined, or preceded by a page break to make it easy to see when a new page begins.

B A scene heading is sometimes referred to as a *slugline*, or *slug*.

C Each element to be lettered—each individual piece of dialogue, caption, sound effect, etc.—is numbered sequentially, with the numbering starting over for each page when applicable. If the writer or editor will be sending a guide to the letterer mapping out the approximate placement of these elements in each panel, they'll be labeled with these numbers to identify them.

D Character names and other indicators are usually written in all caps. Because the letterer will be copying and pasting the dialogue and captions into their design program, having these set off from the text to be lettered—as on separate lines or in separate columns—makes this process easier.

E As mentioned under **Capitalization and Crossbars**, a script might use a lowercase *i* anywhere there should be a slash I, even at the beginning of a sentence, so that the letterer does not have to change these letters from the crossbar version manually.

F Sound effects are set up the same way dialogue is.

G Text that will be bold italic in the final comic might be bold, italicized, underlined, or any combination of the three in a script. Some writers will use all-caps for emphasis, but usually this isn't ideal for the letterer for the reasons discussed under **Capitalization and Crossbars**, even if the final comic will use mixed-case body text with all caps for emphasis.

H Text in parentheses is often used to indicate the type of speech/balloon—off-panel, voiceover, shouting, whispering, etc. (See the **Balloons** section in chapter 4 for an explanation of balloon types.)

I Each balloon gets a new dialogue marker with a new number, even if the same character is continuing to speak.

J Reverse angle brackets are one style that may be used to indicate breath marks. You might also see curly or square brackets, which are the characters for breath marks in some comics fonts.

EDITING TIPS

Dialogue

Although things like word choice and how dialogue is broken up across balloons are primarily the job of the editor and/or writer, it's acceptable for a copyeditor to flag possible balloon issues if they see them. For example:

- An especially long chunk of text that isn't broken up into multiple balloons or captions and it isn't clearly being done for intentional stylistic effect—especially if there are many panels on a page or screen, meaning each one will be relatively small.

- A single balloon that combines separate thoughts, even if it isn't especially long. The general guideline is one idea or thought per balloon. Although this isn't a black-and-white rule, if a character is completely switching gears, it's often appropriate to start a new balloon.

- Similarly, dialogue directed to multiple other characters in a single balloon—for example, "Jack, you go left. Annie, you go right."

- Balloon descriptors that don't seem to match the dialogue—for example, parentheticals that specify a bit of dialogue is meant to be set in an electric balloon when the speech isn't coming through any kind of electronic medium.

Whether these types of issues should be queried or changed directly will depend on the client and your relationship with them. When in doubt, query.

Other Tips

Other things to watch for include the following:

- Does the number of panels indicated in the header match the number of panels described for that page or section? If not, query it.

- If a panel description includes an element that looks like it's meant to be lettered, but the text doesn't appear in the lettering area, query it. It could very well be that "a sign reading 'Enter at Your Own Risk'" is meant to be part of the artwork, but if it's actually meant for the letterer, it will need to be copied or moved into the lettering area with proper formatting to make sure that person sees it.

DOES IT NEED A COPYEDIT?

When figuring out how much a comic can benefit from a dedicated copyediting pass, asking these questions can be helpful.

What are the writer's strengths?
If a writer is great at grammar, spelling, and style, skipping a copyedit is less risky than it might be otherwise. But don't discount the "style" part of that list—someone might be an amazing writer who rarely makes a spelling or grammar mistake, but that doesn't mean they know all the micro-level style points covered in chapter 2. That's why editors and proofreaders exist, and it's usually more efficient to make sure a comic follows a publisher's style guidelines before it goes to the letterer rather than after.

What are the editor's strengths?
If the main editor (or one of their assistants or associates) is also a great copyeditor, it's much less important for a script to go to a separate person for copyediting. That's not to say it never makes sense in these cases—a fresh set of eyes can catch things the writer and editor might have missed, especially if the story is long, dense, or complex.

How much text is there?
A monthly three-panel webcomic probably doesn't need to be copyedited. An epic graphic novel that's hundreds of pages and thousands of words long really should be. For anything in between, you'll have to balance the length with the other factors on this list.

Does the comic have complex elements or a lot of proper nouns?
If a story mentions lots of place names, features dialogue in a real or fictional foreign language, or uses a complicated structure like multiple timelines, the chances of missing an inconsistency or continuity error are greater. Also, the more revision work the writer and editor have done, the "closer" they'll be to the text and the more likely it is they'll miss something.

Is it a translation?
A comic originally published in another language needs more than translation before it's ready for publication. Has it been localized—adapted to read well for its intended audience? Has it been reviewed to make sure the translation is not just correct and clear, but natural? If the editor has a lot to focus on besides grammar and style, letting a copyeditor worry about the mechanics can be helpful. Conversely, if the editor isn't able to do this type of content reviewing and quality assurance work themselves, that's all the more reason to have someone else look at it.

It's important to weigh all these factors against each other and look at the whole picture when evaluating a project. If the writer is top-notch and editor is great at copyediting, but the comic is long or complex, a dedicated copyeditor can still catch lots of small corrections that are easy to make at the script stage but would really add up if the proofreader and letterer have to make them. There's no magic formula, but when in doubt, I recommend including a copyedit if you can fit it into your budget and schedule.

4
PROOFREADING LAYOUTS AND LETTERING

IN THIS CHAPTER:

What Is Lettering?	95
What Is Typesetting?	96
Proofreading Scope	96
Marking Corrections	99
Typography	102
Balloons	107
Captions	118

Proofreading a comic can be a big job. In most cases, the proofreader needs to watch for errors not only in spelling, grammar, formatting, and typography, but also balloon arrangement and styling, consistency between the text and the art, and more.

WHAT IS LETTERING?

A letterer is responsible for not only the literal letters in a comic—the dialogue, captions, and sound effects—but also the balloons and boxes they go into.* Although the writer will generally indicate how dialogue should be broken up across balloons, the letterer will often make decisions here too. It's a collaborative artistic process rather than one person executing another's specific directions.

This chapter focuses on the elements of lettering that are helpful for a proofreader to know. For publications and training programs that go into more depth, see **Resources**.

Most lettering is done digitally these days, using graphics software and fonts designed specifically for comics, but some people still work by hand. This is more common in shorter-form work, like webcomics and newspaper strips.

In addition to lettering that's done entirely on paper and scanned in for publication, there are a variety of hybrid processes. For example, a letterer might start with pencil and paper and then digitally ink over a scan of their work, or they might work fully digitally but hand-draw the letters using a graphics tablet rather than using a premade font.

Proofreaders should be aware that changing the text in a speech balloon or caption is more involved if it's hand-lettered than if it's a font. If it looks like a comic is hand-lettered and the client hasn't said anything about keeping changes to a minimum, it's worth checking whether you should limit your corrections in any way.

---

* As mentioned in chapter 1, letterers working on translated comics often have to use the balloons and boxes from the original, and some sound effects are part of the artwork rather than created by the letterer.

WHAT IS TYPESETTING?

Typesetting generally refers to text placement using a layout program like InDesign rather than lettered by hand or using an illustration program. In comics, this is usually used for text that isn't part of the actual story, like an introductory essay, credits in a gallery of behind-the-scenes artwork, or the marketing copy on the back cover of a published book. There is some gray area here—for example, a full-length letter from one character to another, or a similarly text-heavy element appearing within a story, could be either lettered or typeset. Typeset text may be handled by a designer who is separate from the letterer, especially for a print book at a mainstream publisher.

In addition to the creation process being different for lettered and typeset elements, they might follow different styles. It's common for a publisher to follow default *Chicago* or AP style more closely in typeset text, so it might use solid em dashes instead of double dashes or follow different rules for punctuation surrounding italicized text when it comes to the cover or the front matter of a comic.

Note that some publishers (mainly publishers of comics in translation) typeset their captions and dialogue instead of lettering them, as do some creators.

PROOFREADING SCOPE

Because comics so often don't get a dedicated copyedit, proofreading can include changes that in other types of publishing normally get handled at an earlier stage of production and would be seen as overreach if a proofreader marked them. These changes can include grammar, syntax, word choice, and more. This sort of process isn't ideal, and some letterers will (quite understandably) enforce a cap on the number of changes they will accept, but it's a common reality.

In other cases, a proofreader will be told to limit themselves to things that fall under strict traditional proofreading purview, like indisputable spelling errors and lettering or layout issues. This is why, just as with any type of work, it's important for the client and the proofreader to be on the same page when it comes to scope.

When there's no dedicated copyeditor and the editor doesn't provide a style sheet (see **chapter 2**), it's good practice for the proofreader to create one and turn it in with their finished work.

Sometimes, it's the responsibility of the comic's editor or another staff person to review panels after the letterer has incorporated proofreading corrections to confirm everything has been implemented correctly. Other times, the proofreader will be asked to do this.

What Parts Get Proofread?

A proofreader is mainly concerned with lettered and typeset text. Besides dialogue, captions, and sound effects, this might also include titles and credits, indicia pages (where the publisher and copyright information is listed), tables of contents, introductions, art gallery captions, and other elements. The proofreader is also usually responsible for checking the designed elements like balloons and caption boxes that contain this text.

Lettering

In addition to editorial and typographic issues, comics proofreaders are usually expected to review at least some of the other elements involved in lettering, such as the look of balloons and caption boxes. This chapter gives an overview of some common styles and uses for these elements and errors that can arise.

Reading Order

Balloons and captions should be arranged in a way that makes it clear what path a reader's eye is supposed to take within and between panels. If a proofreader stumbles over reading order, others might too, so they should note this as part of their feedback. Although people who are new to the medium might need to get used to certain practices, like figuring out when to read within a single page and when to cross back and forth across a spread, a good layout will usually be clear even to someone who's never read a comic before.

Artwork

Text that hasn't been placed by the letterer but instead is part of the art should be proofread along with the lettering. But because hand-drawn text is much harder to change than text that uses a digital font, especially if the pages have already been colored, only true errors should be marked in artwork at the proofreading stage. It's not important for a sign in a restaurant window to follow *Chicago Manual of Style* hyphenation rules, but if an attorney is going to work at the Pubic Defender's Office, that should be fixed.

It's also important to watch for possible inconsistencies between the lettering and the text. Does a baseball player have a different number on their jersey than the one mentioned for them in the captions? Is a character's name spelled a different way in dialogue than on the name tag they're wearing? Does someone say they're going to grab one of the apples on the table, but it's actually a bowl of oranges? The mismatch could be on purpose for story reasons, but if not, one or the other will probably need to change.

It's not usually the proofreader's responsibility to review the artwork for other types of consistency or continuity issues. But if you happen to notice something, whether it's a character with an extra finger or a blue house that's mistakenly green in one panel, it never hurts to flag it in case the editor or creator hasn't already spotted it. And some clients do explicitly ask proofreaders to review artwork continuity more thoroughly, so it's always good to check at the outset.

Titles and Logos

Whether they're created by a letterer, an artist, a graphic designer, or someone else in the process, specially designed titles and any logo that contains text should be reviewed carefully. Although these have often gone through many rounds of review, especially in the case of a wordmark that has been or will be trademarked, that doesn't mean they don't contain errors—and a typo in the title of a comic or the name of one of its characters is about as embarrassing as it gets. Additionally, just because it's right in one place doesn't mean its right everywhere, so even if it looks like the front cover, spine, and title page all use the same designed title, the proofreader should still read it letter for letter every time, just in case.

MARKING CORRECTIONS

Different publishers and letterers have different preferences when it comes to how proofreaders should mark their changes. If the proofreader is reviewing PDFs, these preferences might involve:

- using digital stamps or freehand markup vs. using only Acrobat's built-in strikethrough, insert, and replace text tools
- using "sticky note" comments vs. text boxes vs. highlighting with comments
- using different styles or features to distinguish comments and queries from text meant to be inserted

Other markup options include using the comment feature in cloud-based review or filesharing systems and providing corrections as a plain-text list with page and panel numbers. Some clients won't have any preferences at all and will just ask that the proofreader be clear and consistent.

Markup Conventions

As mentioned, most comics are lettered in a design program like Illustrator or Clip Studio rather than typeset in a layout program like InDesign, even if prepress work is done in InDesign. (One exception: Publishers of comics in translation that aren't creating their own balloons and caption boxes might use InDesign for lettering.) Although there are workflows that allow designers to directly import changes marked on a PDF into InDesign to accept or reject them, there isn't an equivalent process in Illustrator.

PROOFREADING SYMBOLS

Some comics proofreaders, creators, and publishers don't use traditional proofreading symbols at all, but here are a few of the ones you're most likely to see—whether they're inserted using digital stamps or freehand markup. Some publishers use the full suite of symbols outlined in *The Chicago Manual of Style*, especially if they also publish prose books.

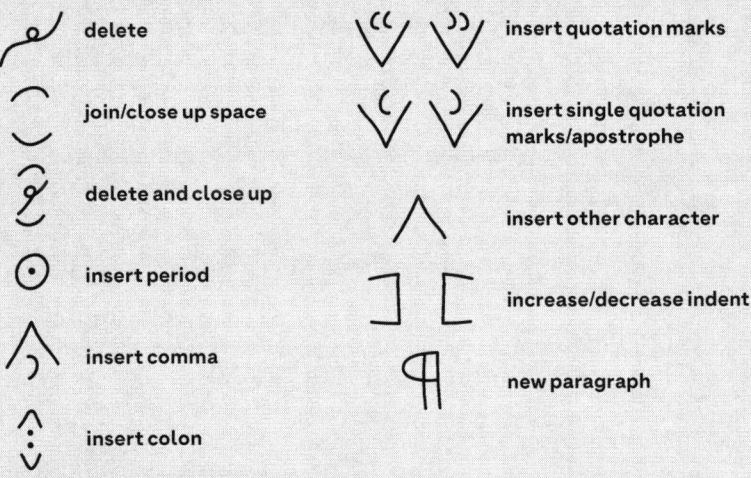

- delete
- join/close up space
- delete and close up
- insert period
- insert comma
- insert colon
- insert quotation marks
- insert single quotation marks/apostrophe
- insert other character
- increase/decrease indent
- new paragraph

Here is one example of a markup style you might see in comics proofreading, combining some traditional symbols with more general PDF notation. If a comic doesn't have a margin on the edge of the page that can accommodate symbols and notes, the markup might go wherever else there's room close to where the change is being made, whether that's in the gutter between panels or in a less busy part of the art.

Because of this, as well as the busy nature of the comic book page or screen, it's much more common than in other types of digital proofreading to use stamps and freehand markup—that is, a style that more closely resembles the traditional markup you'd use on paper proofs. But although editors and typesetters at prose publishers are usually familiar with the traditional proofreading symbols used in that type of markup, that's not always a safe bet in comics. Some symbols, like the one to insert a comma, are pretty comprehensible even to someone who's never seen them before, but marking a space the "traditional" way could result in a letterer inserting a pound symbol in the book. This is part of the instructions a client should ideally provide when it comes to markup preferences.

Proofreading Tools

You don't need any special tools for comics proofreading, but a pen tablet will make your life easier if you do any appreciable amount of freehand markup. These don't have to cost an arm and a leg—if you're just using it for proofreading, you don't need the full suite of features that a digital artist does, and you can find a basic tablet for less than $50. More expensive models have helpful features like built-in screens and more sensitive styluses, but they're usually bulkier, and some need to be plugged into a separate power source. Using a touch-screen tablet can work as well.

One built-in tool I often incorporate into my copyediting and proofreading workflow is the read-aloud feature in Word and Acrobat. Whenever possible, I go through a project one more time, after I've done all my markup, using text to speech to make sure I've caught everything. Unfortunately, this doesn't always work well—or, in some cases, at all—for lettered comics pages because of how the files are set up (plus Acrobat buries the function a bit under Menu>View>Read out loud). Still, it's saved me on several occasions from missing an incorrect character or duplicated word, so it's often worth the hassle.

TYPOGRAPHY

Part of the letterer's job is to create a balloon or caption of the best size and proportions possible for each bit of text and to arrange the text inside in the best way possible. For dialogue, this is often a rough diamond or oval shape, with the text centered, the longest line of text in the middle of the balloon, and the lines above and below getting gradually shorter as they move toward the top and bottom—though this is by no means the style in every comic. Captions tend to be more horizontal and are more likely to use left-aligned text, though you might see centered text in off-panel dialogue captions and left-aligned text for narration, for example.

There are a variety of ways to avoid and fix the issues described in this section, including rebreaking the lines, adjusting the spacing, and reshaping the balloon or box. It's ultimately up to the letterer (or the editor) which one will work best, and it's generally not within the proofreader's purview to suggest changes to things like the design of the balloon shapes. That said, some publishers will specifically ask proofreaders to suggest solutions when it comes to dividing lines of text. At minimum, the proofreader should generally note the acceptable word division options when marking a bad break. For example, if marking HIGHLIGHT-/ED, they would note that the word should either be kept together or broken as HIGH-/LIGHTED.

Word Division

A letterer will generally avoid breaking words across lines when possible, but sometimes it's unavoidable. Word division should follow the guidelines of your style manual and style guide, but the following are common principles:

- break words at the divisions shown in the house dictionary (for example, mar·vel·ous should be broken as mar-/velous or marvel-/ous)

- break hyphenated compounds and compounds formed with en dashes only at the hyphen or dash

- break a word with a prefix or suffix at the place where it connects to the rest of the word
- don't break single-syllable words
- when a word ends in a doubled consonant followed by -ing, it should be broken between the consonants (run-/ning) rather than before the ending (runn-/ing)
- don't create breaks where there are fewer than two characters before or fewer than three characters after the break
- avoid breaking the last word in a balloon, caption, or paragraph
- avoid breaks that create confusion or unintended words (anal-/ysis)
- break a line after, not before, an ellipsis or dash
- don't break a word that immediately precedes or follows an ellipsis or dash
- when a name contains initials, break before or after them (J. R. R./Tolkien, George R. R./Martin), not between (J. R./R. Tolkien, George R./R. Martin)

The proofreader should mark any line divisions that violate these rules as bad breaks unless a publisher has indicated otherwise. Sometimes it's not possible to fix an issue without creating a different or worse issue elsewhere; the letterer and editor can decide which is the lesser of two evils.

Also see the information about hyphen stacks under **Stacks and Rivers**.

Other Line-Break Considerations

Although improper breaks within words are the most glaring, it's also important to look at breaks that occur between words.

As mentioned under **Word Division**, a sentence that includes a double dash or em dash should ideally be broken after the dash, not before. Some people go further and recommend not breaking a line immediately after a dash, either—saying there should be at least one word between the dash and the end of the line unless it's the end of the balloon or caption (as with an interruption or bridging dash). I've seen similar rules applied to ellipses, but less consistently; *Chicago* allows the break to go either before or after ellipses (just not within them, if spaced periods are being used).

It's also good practice to keep emphasized phrases together on the same line. When breaking across lines is necessary, it's best to avoid mixing text that is and isn't emphasized on any one of those lines. (When all the emphasis fits on one line, it's not a problem for roman text to share the line.) It might not be considered a formal bad break if text doesn't follow this guideline, but following it tends to look better.

HEY,
DON'T **WALK
AWAY** FROM
ME!

HEY, DON'T
WALK AWAY
FROM ME!

Widows, Orphans, and Runts

An orphan is the first line of a paragraph that appears by itself at the bottom of a page or column (separated from the rest of the paragraph on the next page). A widow is the last line of a paragraph that appears by itself at the top of a page or column. A runt is a first or final line of a paragraph that consists of a single short word. Many people also use *widow* and *orphan* (or *partial orphan*) to refer to runts.

You're not likely to encounter full-line widows or orphans in comics except in an element like an introduction or creator biography, but runts crop up often in lettering. This is to be expected in balloons because of the diamond shape the text typically follows (as described under **Typography**). A single word at the beginning or end of a speech balloon isn't automatically a problem, though it tends to be more noticeable in captions.

In either case, a publisher may set a threshold of when a word is too short to appear on its own line, or the editor might defer completely to the letterer. Nate Piekos notes in *The Essential Guide to Comic Book Lettering* that he considers a line of three characters or less an orphan or widow (runt). Some publishers and letterers have no minimum length. The examples on this page show short single-word lines that might be considered a widow ("I") and orphan ("It") and how the text could be rebroken to avoid the issue.

(I)
CAN'T SEE
THROUGH THIS
FOG.

I CAN'T
SEE THROUGH
THIS FOG.

DON'T ACT
LIKE YOU KNOW
ANYTHING ABOUT
(IT.)

DON'T
ACT LIKE YOU
KNOW ANYTHING
ABOUT IT.

As mentioned under **Word Division**, it's best to avoid breaking the last word in a balloon or caption across lines when possible. Although this might simply be referred to as a bad break, it's also sometimes called a partial orphan.

Stacks and Rivers

A stack is the same word or character appearing in the same position on multiple lines in a row. A river is a gap running through a block of text that is created by the way the words happen to line up. A ladder is a stack consisting of line-end hyphens used to divide words.

> I DIDN'T KNOW WHAT
> I WAS GOING TO SAY, BUT
> I HAD TO SAY SOMETHING.

It's good to avoid all of these when possible, but as with runts, different publishers will have different thresholds of tolerance. Some don't allow any stacks or rivers, some care about one but not the other, some only care about stacks if they're three lines or more, and some don't care at all.

Leading, Kerning, and Padding

Leading is the space between lines; kerning is the space between letters. Overall, it's up to the letterer and the editor to determine the look of a book, but a proofreader can and should point out places where text seems noticeably tighter or looser than elsewhere or is difficult to read. This is especially the case if, for example, letters are so close together that the *L* and *I* in FLICK look like a *U* or lines are so tight in mixed-case text that a *p* on one line is crashing into a *b* on the next.

The same goes for the amount of space between the text and the border of a balloon or caption box, which might be called the padding, margin, or air. If the margins are uneven or one balloon or box has noticeably more or less air than the others and it isn't being done for stylistic effect, that should be flagged.

Additionally, if a balloon or caption is too close to the edge of the page in a printed comic, it could get lost in the inside gutter around the binding or completely cut off on the outside.

Fonts

Proofreaders should watch that fonts are consistent throughout a comic. The letterer might use a mix of typefaces and sizes for different elements—like captions and dialogue being treated differently, speech for each character having unique styling, or size being used to indicate how loudly someone is talking (see **Size and Volume** in the Balloons section of this chapter). But those differences should usually follow an identifiable pattern.

Ragged Lines

Text is considered to be ragged when the ends of the lines aren't aligned—a paragraph that's left aligned is also called ragged right, and centered text is ragged on both sides. It's generally best to avoid too much variability in the line lengths of ragged text. Of course, "too much" is often subjective, so this can involve developing a good eye for consistency and a familiarity with a particular publisher's or letterer's style.

BALLOONS

Balloons are primarily used to indicate speech and certain other sounds in a comic. Not all comics use balloons, and not all balloons look the same, but they're a dominant and instantly recognizable convention even to people who don't read comics.

Many letterers and publishers follow the rule of thumb that if a character is starting a new thought—for example, switching gears in a conversation or addressing a different character—they should also start a new balloon.

Letterers, editors, and proofreaders should all be on the lookout for any issues with balloons—in an ideal world, between all of them, they'll catch anything that's less than perfect. I'll discuss some common errors in this section, but first I'll go over some of the most common types of balloons and what they're used for.

Balloon Anatomy

padding/air

stroke

tail

LET'S GET A MOVE ON!

BALLOONS OR BUBBLES?

A lot of people in North American comics are very passionate about the fact that the things dialogue goes into are called *balloons*. This isn't the case everywhere in the world—as Shelly Bond notes in *Filth and Grammar*, the three British artists who worked on that book passionately prefer *bubbles*, and you might see it in manga publishing as well. Go with your heart, but know that if you use *bubbles* with a US creator, you might be in for a rant.

Styles and Uses

There will generally be one overall default balloon style for a given comic, but there are infinite possibilities when it comes to creating special styles for different situations, characters, and emotions. Here are some of the most common.

Burst balloon: A spiky, sometimes asymmetrical balloon used to emphasize the dialogue and, in most cases, indicate louder volume. Not all loud dialogue will use burst balloons, but dialogue in burst balloons is almost always meant to be loud. The text inside is often bold italic, enlarged, or both. (Note: A burst balloon is used for dialogue. The term *burst* might be used as shorthand for a burst balloon, but it often refers to a shape containing other types of text—see **Captions, Notes, and Bursts** in chapter 2.)

Electric (a.k.a. radio, broadcast, or comms) balloon: Speech over the phone, TV, radio, and other electronic media often uses scalloped or spiked edges (generally distinct in style from burst balloons) or electric flourishes. Robot characters may use these for speech, or there might be a different robotic balloon style, often with a special font. Although electric balloons sometimes don't have tails in general usage, they usually do if they're being used for a specific "electronic" character like this.

Ice balloon: Icicles or ice cubes on a balloon can indicate the speaker is either literally or figuratively cold.

Inverted-tail balloon: Manga-influenced comics sometimes use a balloon with a tail-shaped cutout to indicate off-panel speech.

Outline balloon: Like a burst balloon, a balloon with an extra outline around it emphasizes the text—which, as in a burst balloon, may be emphasized or enlarged.

Rough balloon: A balloon with rough, jagged edges may be used for distorted speech, such as a monster's dialogue.

Squink: When there's something between the speaker and the reader, like a door, a window, or an entire building or vehicle, the tail of their speech balloon will often end in a little burst called a squink.

Tailless balloon: In Western-style comics, a tailless balloon usually indicates that the speaker isn't visible. It might be used instead of a tail pointing off-panel; instead of a squink for something like a character's dialogue shown over an establishing shot of the spaceship they're traveling in; or even instead of a voice-over caption. On the other hand, you might see this balloon style used when the character *is* in frame for telepathic dialogue—see the next entry. And some comics, especially those influenced by manga, manhua, or manhwa, will use tailless balloons for internal thoughts or even in some contexts for regular dialogue spoken out loud by a visible character (for example, if the character and the balloon are on opposite sides of the panel).

Telepathic balloon: There's no one way to style balloons indicating dialogue "spoken" telepathically. They might be wavy or jagged, or they might have a special color or outline style. Telepathic balloons are often tailless, in which case it's important to make sure it's clear who's speaking—whether through placement, color, other style features, or context (for example, the simple fact that only one character in the comic or scene has that power).

Thought balloon: When a balloon is used to indicate a character's thoughts, it usually uses the stereotypical "bubble" style, with a cloudlike balloon connected to the thinker by circles or ovals. But in modern comics, it's common to see thoughts set in caption boxes instead. (See **Captions, Notes, and Bursts** in chapter 2.)

Wavy, weak, or deflated balloon: A balloon with an uneven, wobbly outline generally indicates unsteadiness in speech, like if a character is disoriented, sleepy, or weak. (As noted in **chapter 2**, capitalization can be used to similar effect.) Wavy balloons are also sometimes used as a stylistic choice for all dialogue for a particular character.

Whisper balloon: Dashed outlines and faded colors are two of the most common ways to indicate whispering, but hardly the only ones. Size and white space can also be used for this purpose.

Again, this is in no way an exhaustive list, and letterers can get creative in infinite other wonderful ways. Letterers Todd Klein and Hassan Otsmane-Elhaou have both made numerous examples and other helpful information available online, Klein on his blog and Otsmane-Elhaou in his newsletter.

Additionally, it's worth noting that I've used oval balloons by default for the examples in this book, but balloons can be any shape—even if they're not for "special" dialogue. The normal style in a comic can be square, lumpy, jagged, polygonal, or anything else that suits the letterer's style and the feel of the story and art (and they don't have to have outlines, either).

Images in Balloons
Sometimes, instead of words or punctuation marks, a balloon will contain artwork or symbols. This could serve any number of uses—for example, to graphically represent what a character is saying or thinking, to indicate the source of an off-panel noise, or to take the place of a grawlix.

Proofreading Balloon Styles
Proofreaders should keep an eye out for potential inconsistencies in style, such as:

- missing styles (for example, a comic uses electric balloons for speech coming through a phone, but one panel uses a regular balloon instead)
- improperly applied styles (for example, a whisper balloon being used when it looks like the character is shouting)
- missing or improperly applied squinks (for example, a comic uses squinks throughout, but one balloon that is coming from the other side of a door doesn't have one—or, conversely, a balloon has a squink even though it originates on the reader's side of the door)

- one or more balloons whose tails don't look like the rest—for example, the base where it connects to the balloon is significantly wider or narrower
- a special balloon type that doesn't look like the others in its category, such as a dashed outline style being used for whispering when the rest of the comic uses faded whisper balloons with solid outlines

Some "inconsistencies," of course, might be deliberate—a tail might look different because it's reflecting a particular type of speech, or different styles of telepathic balloons might be used for different characters. It's always important to think critically, look at the big picture, and ask if you're not sure.

Balloons and Panels

When a balloon is too big to fit entirely inside a panel, it can either stop at the panel border with a hard line (butting balloon), break the border and connect to the gutter space, or overlie the border. As with so many things in this chapter, the choice between these options is up to the letterer and editor, but inconsistencies should be flagged. One comic can use a mix of styles, but if a whole book or scene uses one approach except for a single balloon that's different—and it doesn't seem to be a stylistic choice—it might not be deliberate.

The main thing to avoid is a tangent, where the edge of the balloon just barely touches the border. For more, see **Common Balloon Errors**.

Butting balloon

Border-breaking balloon

Overlapping balloon

Balloon tangent

Joining Balloons

When one character has multiple balloons in a single panel, there are a few formatting options. The letterer might simply draw two or more fully separate balloons. They might butt the balloons up against each other and erase the border where they meet—a style that's generally used when a character is continuing a thought. The place where the two balloons merge is called a *join*.

Another option is to join the balloon bodies with connectors, a style often used when someone else is speaking in between the two comments or when the balloons need to fit around elements of the artwork.

If multiple balloons for a single speaker are joined, whether directly or with connectors, there's only one tail. On the other hand, if multiple people are saying something in unison, you might see a single balloon with multiple tails.

Separate balloons sometimes overlap or even merge with each other even if they're from different speakers—whether to show people talking over each other, to save space, or as a general creative choice. When balloons overlap, there isn't a universal guideline for what goes in front, though if one character is interrupting another, it's common for the interrupter's speech to be on top.

Size and Volume
(and Other Creative Uses of White Space)

The size of text can be used to communicate both the volume and the character of speech in comics. Size can be either absolute, as in the actual point size of the text, or relative, as in the amount of white space in a balloon surrounding it. Volume can also be absolute or relative: One character might be quieter than another because they're speaking more quietly, or they might just be way off in the background.

    White space can also be an overall stylistic choice—a letterer may simply choose to have extra air in all their balloons because that's the look and feel they want. This is particularly common in East Asian–influenced comics, but it's certainly used in Western-style comics as well.

Common Balloon Errors

In general, the proofreader should watch for and identify balloon errors like these, but they're not expected to suggest specific solutions—that falls to the letterer or editor.

Ambiguous, Misplaced, and Missing Tails

Keep a sharp eye out for balloons that seem to be assigned to the wrong speaker, or where it's hard to tell who the tail is pointing to. Usually, a tail should point to a character's mouth (or wherever it is they're speaking from).

Crossed Tails

Outside some extremely rare, deliberate cases, balloon tails should never overlap each other.

Tangents

In the context of balloons, a tangent is a border or tail that butts right up against another line—whether the edge of a panel (see the example on page 115), another balloon, a caption box, a sound effect, or something in the art. This is a design no-no. Either the balloon should overlap or underlie the other element, or there should be a comfortable margin between the two.

Tangents also occur in other contexts that are the responsibility of the artist.

Merging Text
When balloons are merged and the text blocks are close together, the reader may initially think that it's a single block and they're supposed to read all the way across both balloons. The letterer can address this by increasing the spacing around the text or moving one balloon up or down a little to offset the lines of text.

Plane/Depth Errors
Sometimes, a letterer will place a balloon behind some element of the artwork, like a character's hand or a flying weapon. This technique can both save space and add visual interest, but it should generally follow consistent spatial logic. For example, if part of a balloon is behind a character's head, a different part of that same balloon shouldn't be in front of part of their body or a piece of furniture that's further in the foreground ("closer" to the reader).

CAPTIONS

Most of the important things a proofreader needs to know about captions—such as the way quotation marks are used across a continuing series of voiceover caption boxes—are covered in the **Captions, Notes, and Bursts** section of chapter 2 and the **Typography** section of this chapter. But here are a few other things to keep in mind.

Common Caption Errors

Inconsistent Alignment
Whether captions are left-aligned or centered, the style should be consistent. One caveat: A comic may use different alignment styles depending on whether a caption is narration, off-panel dialogue, or a thought.

Incorrect Style Application
Besides alignment, the letterer may use different fonts, colors, icons, box shapes, or other styles to distinguish different types of captions—not only narration, off-panel dialogue, and thoughts, but also different characters. Especially if there are a lot of these styles, it can be easy for one to slip through that's formatted incorrectly, whether that means the entirely wrong style has been applied or the correct style has been applied incorrectly (for example, a character icon is missing when it should be present or vice versa).

Missing and Misplaced Footnotes
When an asterisk appears in a speech balloon or caption, make sure that there's a corresponding footnote—and that its placement follows the publisher's guidelines. A footnote should generally be as close as possible to the reference, and the publisher may specifically require that it appear in the same panel.

Missing Time and Place Captions
Not all comics use a caption to establish the time or place every time there's a change of scene, but as with everything, if this format is used, it should be used consistently.

Tangents
Tangents can be an issue with captions just as they are with balloons. In addition to watching the margins between caption boxes and the edges of panels, the proofreader should keep an eye out for any lines in the art that seem to extend or awkwardly touch the caption box borders.

APPENDIX: SAMPLE STYLE SHEET

A style sheet is an important tool in just about any type of editing or publishing. As described in **chapter 2**, it lists all the style and spelling decisions for an individual comic or series that either supplement or override the main style guide or style manual that the comic is following.

If a comic gets a dedicated copyedit, the copyeditor should create the style sheet as part of that process. The editor and/or writer should review it and make any needed adjustments, and then whoever is directing the proofreader should send the style sheet to them along with the lettered pages. The proofreader will use the style sheet for reference in their work and, if appropriate, make additions—whether that's a spelling that wasn't accounted for or special balloon styles for certain characters (more on that in a minute). If there is no dedicated copyedit, either the editor or the proofreader will create the style sheet.

As I did in **chapter 3**, I've used *client* throughout this appendix as shorthand for whoever will be reviewing copyedits and making decisions on the script—whether that's a proofreading manager working with a freelance copyeditor, a writer working with an in-house editor, or someone else.

Time Pirates of the Orion Nebula
Style Sheet

References

- ABC Publisher Style Guide
- *The Chicago Manual of Style*, 18th edition
- Merriam-Webster online dictionary (merriam-webster.com)

Characters A

Maris, 28, she/her
Jax, 24, they/them
Nico, 19, he/him
Sol, ship's computer (square balloons with robotic font) B

Style

- Use true em dashes (—), not double dashes (--)
- Text in breath marks is not italicized
- Don't use a comma with "like" as an approximator ("It was like 50 feet tall!")
- Do use a comma with "too" ("He drives a hard bargain, too")

Spelling

General C
'cuz (for "because")
hijinks
spacetime
time travel (n.), time-travel (v.)
worshipped

Locations D
Cassini (colony)
Ganymede
Terra
Trapezium Station

Other Proper Nouns
Galactic Council
Sirius, the (ship)

A Characters: Some copyeditors, proofreaders, and clients prefer to include character details like ages, pronouns, and roles on the style sheet; others prefer a simple list of names. Even if this type of information isn't listed on the final style sheet, a copyeditor or proofreader will want to keep track of it in their personal notes to make sure everything is consistent throughout the work.

B Lettering styles: It might or might not be the proofreader's responsibility to document balloon and caption styles on a style sheet. A complete list is usually not expected, but it's a good idea to ask the client as part of outlining the scope of work. But as with character details, even if this information doesn't end up on the style sheet, the proofreader should keep track of the styles and check that they're consistently applied throughout the comic. In this example, I've included a description just for the character whose speech balloons are different from the default style, but you might also document different box shapes or text alignments for captions depending on whether they're for narration or off-panel dialogue.

C Common nouns: Any word or name that meets one of the following criteria should generally be documented on a style sheet:

- its spelling or style isn't covered by the house style guide, style manual, or dictionary

- it goes against a house style rule (for example, *The Chicago Manual of Style* would normally use the spelling "worshiped"—the manual doesn't double a final consonant that follows a single vowel if it's not part of the stressed syllable—but the writer prefers "worshipped")

- it has more than one acceptable spelling listed in the house dictionary (Merriam-Webster lists both "hijinks" and "high jinks," but the writer prefers the first one)

- it goes against the house dictionary's listed spelling(s) (Merriam-Webster lists the spelling "space-time," but the publisher prefers to spell it "spacetime")

D **Proper nouns:** All proper nouns, like the real moon Ganymede and the fictional Galactic Council, should generally be listed on the style sheet. One potential challenge is that if the person creating or revising a style sheet is a proofreader rather than a copyeditor and the comic is lettered in all-caps text, it won't always be possible for them to tell what's a proper noun and what's not. In these cases, it usually doesn't make sense to query during the course of the proofread because it doesn't actually affect the work, but the ambiguity should be noted either on the style sheet or in the final project notes to the client. Although the answer might not be relevant to the end reader when it comes to the comic book itself, it could come up on cover copy or other marketing text, or in mixed-case text in a future book in the same series.

GLOSSARY

arc: a storyline that usually spans multiple installments (issues, episodes, etc.) of a comic

artist: an umbrella term that can refer to a penciller, inker, colorist, cover artist, or any other artist working on a comic, including one person filling multiple roles

balloon: a shape that contains text, symbols, or images and is most often used to communicate speech, thought, or emotion in a comic

bandes dessinées: French-language comics originating in France, Belgium, or sometimes Québec

bleed: either the placement of artwork extending all the way to the edge of a page or screen or the outermost margin of that artwork that may be cut off in printing

breath marks: a set of outward-radiating lines that frame sounds like sighs, grunts, coughs, and other vocalizations that aren't speech

burst: a spiky shape containing text—usually text other than dialogue, though this term may also be used to mean a burst balloon

burst balloon: a usually spiky balloon used to emphasize dialogue

cartoonist: a term for some creators who write, draw, and letter their own comics (especially comic strips and single-panel cartoons)

caption: lettered text that appears in a box or is otherwise set off from the artwork and balloons

character bible: a document compiling character-related details for a book or series

comms balloon—see electric balloon

colorist: an artist who applies color to the black-and-white artwork created by the inker

copyediting: reviewing text for grammar, punctuation, spelling, formatting, and consistency; may also include word choice, sentence flow, fact-checking, and other aspects

crossbar I: a capital I with horizontal bars at the top and bottom (I), used for the personal pronoun and, depending on the publisher, other limited cases

designer: generally, someone who creates design elements that aren't part of the comic itself, such as the jacket and front and back matter of a printed book

digital comic: either a digital version of a print-style comic or an umbrella term describing any comic published in an electronic format

double dash: two hyphens (--) used in place of a solid em dash (—) to indicate a break in speech

e-comic—see digital comic

editor: in comics, someone who might acquire or commission a project, develop and edit the story with the writer, copyedit, art-direct, manage editorial freelancers, or all of the above

electric balloon: a balloon used for speech over the phone, TV, radio, or other electronic medium, often featuring scalloped edges, spikes, or "electric" flourishes

event: a big storyline, usually taking place across multiple series from a publisher

flatter: a person who prepares inked panels for the colorist by mapping out the areas where color will go

graphic novel: usually refers to a book-length comic telling a single story

gutter: the space outside and between the panels, or the part of a printed page closest to the binding

grawlix: a series of symbols used to obscure profanity (ex: #@$%)

house style: a publisher's collective style preferences and editing or proofreading guidelines, usually documented in a style guide

kerning: the spacing between letters

ice balloon: a balloon with icicles or other cold imagery used to indicate the speaker is literally or figuratively cold

indicia: details about the publication and publisher, often appearing alongside the copyright notice for a work

inker: an artist who uses the penciller's artwork as a guide to create the line art for a comic

inset: a panel within a panel

inverted-tail balloon: a balloon with a tail-shaped cutout used to indicate off-panel speech in manga and manga-influenced comics

ladder: a series of line-end hyphens appearing on successive lines

leading: the spacing between lines of text

letterer: a person who places the writer's text in the comic and creates the balloons, caption boxes, and other shapes that contain it, as well as sound effects and, sometimes, logos

locator: a caption indicating where a scene is taking place (sometimes used more broadly to mean any caption indicating place, time, or both)

manga: comics originating in Japan

manhua: comics originating in China

manhwa: comics originating in Korea

obscenicon—see grawlix

orphan: the first line of a paragraph that appears by itself at the bottom of a page or column or the final line of a paragraph consisting of a single short word

outline balloon: a balloon with an extra outline around it used to emphasize text

panel: a single frame within a comic

penciller: an artist who interprets the script into preliminary artwork

prepress/production artist: a person who combines and prepares artwork and lettering for print or digital publication

proofreading: reviewing lettered panels or typeset materials for grammar, punctuation, spelling, formatting, consistency, and lettering or typesetting errors

profanitype—see grawlix

radio balloon—see electric balloon

river: a continuous gap running between words across multiple lines in a block of text

rough balloon: a balloon with rough, jagged edges used for distorted speech

roughs: draft sketches laying out panels and artwork

runt: the first or last line of a paragraph consisting of a single short word

script: a document mapping out the art direction and text to be lettered for a comic

SFX—see sound effect

slash I: a capital I without crossbars, used for most placements in all-caps comics

slugline (slug): a short heading in a script denoting the setting of a scene

splash: a large "hero" panel

squink: a small burst at the end of a balloon tail that indicates the sound is coming from the other side of a wall, window, or other barrier

spread: two facing pages in a print (or print-style) publication

sound effect: text indicating a sound that isn't part of dialogue

story bible: a document compiling story-related details for a book or series, such as settings, in-world mechanics, and languages; characters may be included in this or documented separately in a character bible

style guide: a document that lays out the preferred style for a specific company, imprint, or brand; might also refer to a style manual or style sheet

style manual: a reference book that lays out a system of style guidelines

style sheet: a document that lays out the preferred style for a single book or series

tail: the part of a balloon pointing from the text area to the speaker or origin of sound

telepathic balloon: any balloon used for telepathic speech; often tailless and may use wavy edges or a special outline

tangent: two lines of artwork or lettering butting right up to each other

tier: a row of panels

voiceover: in comics, this term might describe nondiegetic narration, diegetic dialogue spoken by an off-panel character, or a character's thoughts set in captions

webcomic: a comic made specifically for the internet and published on a website and/or app; usually refers to comics that don't follow the page format of a traditional print comic and are released one episode, strip, or panel at a time

webtoon: a vertical-scrolling type of webcomic meant to be read on a smartphone

whiskers—see breath marks

widow: the last line of a paragraph that appears by itself at the top of a page or column or the first line of a paragraph consisting of a single short word

writer: in comics, the person who comes up with the story concept and worldbuilding and/or writes the script

For a more detailed discussion about the definitions of comics and graphic novels; digital comics, webcomics, and webtoons; and copyediting and proofreading, see the **Notes on Terminology** section in the introduction. For the distinctions between style manuals, style guides, and style sheets, see **Style References** in chapter 2. For the question of "speech balloon" versus "speech bubble," see the **Balloons or Bubbles?** sidebar in chapter 4.

RESOURCES

I have direct experience with most of the books, organizations, and courses listed here, but some I'm including based on others' recommendations, so I can't speak to every single listing firsthand. These lists are meant as a helpful starting place and don't pretend to be exhaustive.

BOOKS, BLOGS, AND MORE

Comics Editing and Style

- Shelly Bond, *Filth and Grammar: The Comic Book Editor's (Secret) Handbook* (Off Register Press, 2022)
- Jan Mitsuko Cash, *Editing Manga: Working with Translations in a Visual Medium* (Editorial Freelancers Association, 2023)
- Comic Book FX: The Comic Book Sound Effect Database, comicbookfx.com
- Comic Book Script Archive, comicbookscriptarchive.com
- Comics Experience Script Archive, comicsexperience.com/scripts
- Todd Klein, "Preparing Comics Scripts for Editing," kleinletters.com/Blog/preparing-comics-scripts-for-lettering
- Scott McCloud, *Making Comics: Storytelling Secrets of Comics, Manga, and Graphic Novels* (William Morrow, 2006)
- Nate Piekos, "Comic Script Basics," blambot.com/pages/comic-script-basics
- Kenny Porter, "How to Easily Format a Comic Book Script" (2019), portercomics.com/blog/2019/7/6/how-to-easily-format-a-comic-book-script

General Editing and Style

- Renni Browne and Dave King, *Self-Editing for Fiction Writers* (William Morrow, 2004)
- BuzzFeed News, the BuzzFeed Style Guide, bzfd.it/styleguide
- Bryan Garner, *The Chicago Guide to Grammar, Usage, and Punctuation* (University of Chicago Press, 2016)
- Jonathon Green, Green's Dictionary of Slang, greensdictofslang.com
- Louise Harnby, "How to Convey Accents in Fiction Writing: Beyond Phonetic Spelling," on louiseharnbyproofreader.com/blog
- Jordan Kantey, "How to Write Accents and Dialects: 6 Tips," nownovel.com/blog/how-to-write-accents-dialects
- Gretchen McCulloch, *Because Internet: Understanding the New Rules of Language* (Riverhead Books, 2020)
- Katharine O'Moore-Klopf, Copyeditors' Knowledge Base, kokedit.com/ckb.php
- Crystal Shelley, conscious and inclusive language resources, rabbitwitharedpen.com/conscious-language
- Amy J. Schneider, *The Chicago Guide to Copyediting Fiction* (University of Chicago Press, 2023)
- *Strong Language: A Sweary Blog About Swearing*, stronglang.wordpress.com
- Kia Thomas, *A Very Sweary Dictionary* (self-published, 2020)
- Karen Yin, *The Conscious Style Guide* (Little, Brown Spark, 2024)

Style Manuals

- *The Associated Press Stylebook*, apstylebook.com
- *The Chicago Manual of Style*, chicagomanualofstyle.org

Lettering

- Blambot (Nate Piekos)
    - Blambot website, blambot.com
    - *The Essential Guide to Comic Book Lettering* (Image, 2022)
- Comicraft (Richard Starkings and John Roshell)
    - Balloon Tales website, balloontales.com
    - *Comic Book Lettering the Comicraft Way* (Comicraft, 2003)
- Todd Klein
    - Blog, kleinletters.com/Blog
- Hassan Otsmane-Elhaou
    - *Lettering List* newsletter, buttondown.com/hassanoe
    - Strip Panel Naked, youtube.com/@StripPanelNaked

Other Comics Creation and Publishing Topics

- Brian Michael Bendis, *Words for Pictures: The Art and Business of Writing Comics and Graphic Novels* (Watson-Guptill, 2014)
- Shelly Bond, *Fast Times in Comic Book Editing* (Off Register Press, 2023)
- Will Eisner, *Comics and Sequential Art* (W. W. Norton & Company, 2008)
- Will Eisner, *Graphic Storytelling and Visual Narrative* (W. W. Norton & Company, 2008)
- David Harper, SKTCHD *Off Panel* podcast, sktchd.libsyn.com
- Scott McCloud, *Reinventing Comics* (William Morrow, 2000)
- Scott McCloud, *Understanding Comics: The Invisible Art* (William Morrow, 1993)
- Greg Pak and Fred Van Lente, *Make Comics Like the Pros* (Watson-Guptill, 2014)
- *PanelxPanel* online magazine, panelxpanel.gumroad.com
- Chris Schweizer, "Tangents," schweizercomics.com/tangents
- Matthew Shifrin, "Panel by Panel: Comic Book Access for the Blind," *Future Reflections* 35, no. 3 (fall 2016)
- Spin Weave and Cut, Accessible Comics for the Blind Project, spinweaveandcut.com/blind-accessible-comics
- Reimena Yee, the Creator's Guide to Comics Devices, comicsdevices.com

EDUCATION

Comics-Related Training

- California College of the Arts, MFA in Comics, comics.cca.edu
- Comicraft, "Lettering Comic Books with Adobe Illustrator," balloontales.com/online-course
- Comics Experience, comicsexperience.com
- Filth and Grammar Online, offregister.press/fgonline
- The Kubert School, kubertschool.edu
- Minneapolis College of Art and Design, Comic Art program, mcad.edu
- Portland State University, Comics Studies program, pdx.edu/comics-studies
- University of California Los Angeles Extension program, Comics and Graphic Novels coursework, uclaextension.edu

General Editing and Proofreading Training

- ACES: The Society for Editing, aceseditors.org/training
- Columbia Publishing Course, journalism.columbia.edu/cpc-ny
- Denver Publishing Institute, liberalarts.du.edu/publishing
- Editorial Freelancers Association, the-efa.org/education
- Editors Canada, editors.ca/professional-development
- Emerson College copyediting certificate, emerson.edu
- NYU Summer Publishing Institute, sps.nyu.edu
- University of California San Diego copyediting certificate, extendedstudies.ucsd.edu

PROFESSIONAL ASSOCIATIONS AND DISCUSSION SPACES

Professional groups are a great way to connect with other people who do what you do, develop your skills, and find potential work. The three most prominent general associations for editors and proofreaders in North America are ACES: The Society for Editing, the Editorial Freelancers Association, and Editors Canada. There are also lots of locally and regionally based groups—both independent associations like the Professional Editors Network and the Northwest Editors Guild and chapters of national organizations. And there are groups based around specific identities and specialties.

Associations for writers and artists include the National Cartoonists Society, the Society of Children's Book Writers and Illustrators, the Science Fiction and Fantasy Writers Association, and the Horror Writers Association.

There are also a wide variety of online communities that don't require paid membership, including the Comic Book Editors Alliance on Facebook. I've assembled a general list of editor-focused groups on my website.

For networking in person, you can't beat conferences and conventions. Many of the associations mentioned here hold annual conferences. For comics-specific events, check out the comic cons and fan conventions happening in your city.

INDEX

A

abbreviations 41, 61, 85–86
acronyms and initialisms 39, 49, 87
accent marks 61, 75
accents and dialects 72
accessibility 26, 37
artwork 62–63, 68, 98, 113

B

bad breaks 102–103
balloons 107–118
    bubbles vs. 108
    common errors 113–114, 117–118
    joining 115–116, 118
    overlapping 114–115, 116
    panel borders and 114–115
    quotation marks in 52
    in scripts 88–91
    spacing and 106
    tails 66, 107, 109–111, 114, 116, 117
    translation and 17, 99
    types 108–113
    typography and 102–107
bold text. *See* emphasis
brands 73
breath marks 35, 59, 69, 88, 90
bubbles. *See* balloons
bursts 68, 108

C

capitalization 35–40, 50, 77, 124
    accessibility and 37
    crossbar I and 36–37, 87
    drop caps 37
    of initial "the" 38
    internal 37, 39, 74–75
    of personal names 37–38, 74–75
    repeated sounds and 46
    in scripts 35–36, 87, 88–89
    small caps 39
    title case 39–40
captions 65–68
    common errors 118–119
    footnotes 68
    narration and 51–52, 59, 65–67, 102
    off-panel speech and 51–52, 66
    punctuation in 51–52
    in scripts 88–89
    signs, letters, and screens 68
    special shapes 68
    time and place 40, 67, 119

censor bars 70
compounds 46, 75–76, 102
conscious language 24, 25
continuity 83, 98
copyright 71, 73
crossbar I 36–37, 87, 88–89
currency 56

D

diacritical marks 61, 75
dialogue. *See* speech
digital comics 11–12. *See also* webcomics
direct address 38, 43
drop caps 37

E

emails 68
emphasis
    balloon styles 108, 110
    punctuation and 48, 58–59, 65
    in scripts 85, 88–89
    text treatment 57–59, 104, 108

F

family terms 37–38
file types 27–28, 85
fonts
    accessibility 26
    glyphs 36, 45, 56, 90
    proofreading 106–107

footnotes 42, 52–53, 60, 68, 119
foreign languages 60–61
formatting (text) 57–65
    alignment 102, 107, 119
    emphasis 57–59
    fractions 56
    italics 59–60, 61
    non-English text 60–61
    scripts 62, 82–83, 88–90
    titles of works 64

G

graphic novels, defined 11
grawlixes (%#&@) 70, 113

H

hashtags 37
hesitation noises 35, 69
house style, defined 32

I

i (letter). *See* crossbar I; slash I
inclusive language, 24, 25
initials 49, 74–75, 103
interruptions 45, 51, 116
italics 58, 59–60, 61

K

kerning 106
kinship names 37–38

L

leading 106
lettering
    defined 95
    process 16–17, 95, 99
    typography and 102–107
letters as letters 59, 62
line breaks 102–104
localization 24, 93
logos 71, 98–99
lyrics 71

M

manga, manhua, and manhwa
    balloons 17, 109, 111
    punctuation 44, 47, 69
    sound effects 63
markup. *See* proofreading marks
mathematical symbols 56–57
military terms 37–38, 55, 61
music 71

N

names. *See* proper nouns
narration 51–52, 59, 65–67, 102
non-English text 60–61
nonword vocalizations 35, 59, 69

numbers 54–57
    decades 39, 41, 55
    decimals 55
    fractions 56
    measurements 54, 56–57
    ordinals 54, 56
    percentages 54, 56
    plurals of 39
    ranges 44, 57
    Roman numerals 36, 55
    symbols and 56–57
    times 55, 67

O

off-panel sounds
    dialogue 51–52, 66, 85, 109, 111
    other sounds 113
onomatopoeias 62–63, 69. *See also* sound effects
orphans (typography) 104–105

P

panels
    proofreading 114–115, 117–118, 119
    in scripts 86, 88–89
plurals 39, 62
possessives 61
profanity 63, 70–71, 75, 113
proofreading marks 99–101

proper nouns
    acronyms 39, 49, 87
    brands and companies 41, 73
    italics and 59
    personal names 37–38, 39, 61, 73–75, 103
    style sheets and 122–124
publisher tips
    accessibility 26
    commas 43
    copyediting 92–93
    editorial freelancers 29
    numbers 55
    spelling 77–78
    style guides 33
punctuation 40–53
    acronyms and 49
    breath marks and 69
    bridging 45, 48
    capitalization and 39
    in captions 51–52, 67
    combining 52–53
    common errors 53
    emphasis and 58–59
    italics and 59
    non-English speech and 60
    plurals and 62
    sound effects and 62–63
    speech and 49–50, 51–52

R
ranks 37–38, 61
rivers (typography) 105–106
runts (typography) 104–105

S
sarcasm 35
scope
    copyediting 22, 62–63, 82–84
    proofreading 27, 62–63, 74, 96–99
shouting. *See* volume indicators
singing 59, 71
slash I 36–37, 87, 89
slang 76
slurs 70–71, 76
software
    art 17
    editing 17, 85
    lettering 17, 95, 99
    proofreading 99
    layout 17, 96
sound effects 17, 62–63, 68, 88–89
speech
    accents and dialects 72
    emphasis in 57–59
    non-English 60–61
    numbers in 54
    off-panel 51–52, 66, 85, 109, 111

(speech, cont.)
    punctuation and 49–50, 51–52
    stammering 46
    telepathic 111
    See also balloons; volume indicators
spelling 62, 72–78, 121–124
squinks 110, 113
stammering 46
style guides 31–32, 33
style manuals 31–32, 34
style sheets 21, 22, 31–33, 74, 121–124
subscript and superscript 42, 56
symbols
    breath marks 69
    copyright and trademark 73
    grawlixes (%#&@) 70, 113
    icons 66, 119
    musical notes 71
    numbers and 56–57
    proofreading marks 99–101
    use in balloons 113
    wave dashes (~) 47
    See also punctuation

T

tangents 117–118, 119
text alignment 102, 107, 119
text messages 68
thoughts 67, 111, 112
titles, personal 37–38, 61
titles of works 39–40, 41, 59, 64
trademarks 38, 73
translation 17, 34, 60–61, 93

U

URLs 37
usernames 37

V

volume indicators
    balloons 108, 112, 116–117
    capitalization 35
    font 58–59, 106–107, 108
    punctuation 48–49, 49
    in scripts 86, 89
    size 108, 110, 112, 116–117

W

webcomics
    defined 11–12
    style 34, 47, 66, 69
whispering. *See* volume indicators
widows (typography) 104–105
word division 102–103
words as words 59
workflow 16–20, 27–28

ABOUT THE AUTHOR

Madeleine Vasaly is a developmental editor, copyeditor, proofreader, and consultant with over a decade of experience in publishing. Her comics background includes a temporary stint at DC Comics as a full-time proofreader in addition to freelance work for DC, IDW, Tapas, Yen Press, and other publishers. She has proofread and copyedited series, one-shots, anthologies, graphic novels, and collected editions across all age ratings and created company-wide style guides for publishers.

Outside her work in comics, Madeleine has edited and proofread hundreds of prose books and countless articles for online newsrooms. She's also the co-head and senior editor of the online magazine and community organization Twin Cities Geek and has served on the board of the Professional Editors Network. She's a member of ACES: The Society for Editing, the Editorial Freelancers Association, and the Minnesota Book Publishers Roundtable.

Learn more at madeleinevasaly.com.